INSTRUCTOR'S MANUAL WITH TEST BANK

MANAGERIAL ECONOMICS
Economic Tools for Today's Decision-Makers

Third Edition

Paul G. Keat
Philip K. Y. Young

Prentice Hall
Upper Saddle River, New Jersey 07458

Acquisitions editor: Rod Banister
Associate editor: Gladys Soto
Project editor: Joan Waxman
Manufacturer: Integrated Book Technology

Printed in the United States of America

10 9 8 7 6 5 4 3 2 1

ISBN 0-13-016994-3

Prentice-Hall International (UK) Limited, *London*
Prentice-Hall of Australia Pty. Limited, *Sydney*
Prentice-Hall Canada Inc., *Toronto*
Prentice-Hall Hispanoamericana, S.A., *Mexico*
Prentice-Hall of India Private Limited, *New Delhi*
Prentice-Hall of Japan, Inc., *Tokyo*
Prentice-Hall (Singapore) Pte Ltd
Editora Prentice-Hall do Brasil, Ltda., *Rio de Janeiro*

Table of Contents

The authors wish to thank Georgia Lessard of the Instructional Design & Support Center at Thunderbird, The American Graduate School of International Management, for preparing this manual in camera-ready format.

OVERVIEW OF THE SOFT DRINK INDUSTRY

Following is a brief overview of the soft drink industry written in a style that might have been used by Bob Burns in the meeting of the Board of Directors. In fact, we were going to include this in Chapter 1 of the text, but the editors suggested that we present this in the instructor's manual. You can always get updated numbers and current activities on this industry from *Beverage World*, *Beverage Industry*, and *Beverage Digest*. Also, *Value Line* and *Standard and Poor's Industrial Surveys* provide good overviews of this industry.

OUTLOOK FOR THE INDUSTRY

The soft drink is America's number one beverage. In 1998, Americans consumed more soft drinks per capita (49% of all gallons consumed) than any other beverage. The table in Slide #1 shows the per capita consumption of various categories of liquids from 1997 to 1998.

Another way to view the importance of soft drinks is to note that in terms of retail receipts in 1998, this product accounted for 29% of the $187 billion beverage market. Beer tied with soft drinks at 29%, followed by spirits 18%; fruit beverages 9.3%; wine 9.3%; and bottled water 2.8%.[1] Notice in particular in Slide #1 that only bottled water actually increased as a percentage of the total between the two years (10.7% to 12.2%). All other categories either decreased slightly or remained constant.

Because of the steady upward trend in the consumption of soft drinks—to the point where it is America's most popular form of beverage—we are very positive about the present and future prospects of the soft drink industry. For example, according to a recent report in *Standard and Poor's Industry Surveys* as of November 26, 1998:

> Soft drinks remain the beverage of choice among the nation's consumers. In 1997, soft drinks accounted for more than one of every four drinks consumed in America, up from one in five a little over a decade ago. Annual per-capita soft drink consumption continues to grow at a low single-digit pace. (p. 12, Foods and Beverage Survey)

However, it is important to note that despite these increases, the U.S. beverage industry has become quite mature, growing in step with the overall population. The growth in the soft drink industry was slightly below the pace of the total beverage market. Nevertheless, the 1.7% annual increase in U.S. soft drink sales volume during 1998 was respectable given the intensifying competitive challenges facing the industry. Competition is coming from the increased popularity of non-carbonated beverages such as bottled water, iced tea, specialty coffees, and fruit-flavored drinks.

MARKET SIZE AND STRUCTURE

The consumption of soft drinks at a rate of about 56.1 gallons per capita per year translates into annual retail sales of $54.3 billion in 1998. This means that a one percent market share represents over $500 million in revenue! Of course, Coca-Cola and Pepsi-Cola dominate the U.S. market. In 1998, the "Red Team" and the "Blue Team" held 44.5% and 31.4% of the market, respectively. Slide #2 depicts the

---

[1] *Beverage World*, May 1999, p. 70.

overwhelming presence of these two firms in the soft drink market. The strength of Coca-Cola and Pepsi-Cola is also reflected in the American preference for cola drinks. Slide #3 shows that colas comprise about two-thirds of all soft drinks consumed. Although the data are not current, other industry reports indicate the trend to be essentially the same: colas continue to dominate the soft drink market.

A key feature of the soft drink industry is the bottling franchise.[2] Major companies such as Coca-Cola and Pepsi-Cola produce the soft drink in concentrated form. This "concentrate" is then sold to bottling franchises that add the carbonated water, bottle the product, and distribute the output to outlets in their territories. Until the early 1950s, most of the franchises were owned and operated by independent bottlers throughout the country. Only a small number were actually held by the major producers of the concentrate.

A major trend over the past 40 years or so has been the decline of the independent bottling company. In 1949, there were nearly 7,000 bottling plants in the United States producing about $860 million (wholesale) worth of soft drinks. By 1986, the number of plants had fallen to 1,336, but their total output was worth $21 billion at the wholesale level. A 1990 study indicated that the number of plants had fallen to 807, but their total output was worth $27.5 billion. By 1998, the number dropped further to fewer than 500.

In addition, many of the remaining plants have been consolidated by multiple franchise operations (MFO), defined in the industry as any company that owns two or more bottling plants. In 1986, 200 MFOs (also called "headquarter companies") accounted for 84% of all U.S. soft drink volume. Most of the consolidation by the headquarter companies has been done by Coca-Cola and Pepsi-Cola. For example, in 1978 Coca-Cola's U.S. bottling system had 370 bottling operators, which has now shrunk to less than 100, and the company expects that this number will decline further. Thus, in the soft drink industry, the Red Team and the Blue Team are now dominant players in bottling as well as in the making of the concentrate.

According to the 1998 *S&P Industry Survey*, the U.S. bottling industry is continuing its ongoing consolidation of the past two decades. Size is becoming crucial in the beverage bottling business, as it enables companies to reduce per-unit operating costs over a greater sales base. In order to compete in today's market, companies must invest in efficiency-enhancing technology capable of producing large volume output. Moreover, consolidation reduces operating expenses and helps improve the industry's pricing flexibility.

MANUFACTURING, PACKAGING, TRANSPORTATION, AND DISTRIBUTION

The ingredients in a soft drink account for only about 5% of its retail price. The rest of the cost is made up of money spent for packaging materials, bottling, transportation, and advertising promotion.

Manufacturing. Manufacturing technology has improved tremendously in recent years. As a case in point, in the 1930s an efficient bottler could produce about 15,000 cases of soft drink per year. Today, this volume can be produced in five hours with a line crew of four people. In fact, manufacturing costs make

---

[2] Notes to Instructors: We decided to focus solely on the packaged soft drink industry. Soft drinks are also produced as fountain syrup and distributed to eating and drinking establishments. This aspect of the industry is not dealt with in the various situations throughout the text.

up only about 6% of the total cost of production. Nonetheless, bottlers continue to seek new ways to reduce manufacturing costs further.

One recent effort involves the use of vertical integration. Certain plants have established their own facility for manufacturing plastic bottles right next to the bottling plant. The benefits of this move are lower cost of this packaging medium as well as quality control and continuity of supply. On the other hand, this option involves a considerable capital expenditure, and the technology in plastic bottle production is constantly changing. Moreover, any bottler that chooses to undertake its own manufacturing of the bottles must constantly measure its efficiency with those of packaging vendors. If this aspect of production is not carefully managed, it may not yield significant savings compared to the purchasing of the bottles from the outside.

Packaging. Over the past decade or so, the industry has witnessed a major shift in its form of packaging. Up until the mid-seventies, the returnable glass bottle was the primary packaging medium. In 1978, the can became the #1 form of packaging. Also in this year, the plastic bottle was introduced, and by 1998 plastics slightly outpaced cans. As Slide #4 illustrates, plastics are 50.9% and cans are 48.3% of the total market.

Transportation and Distribution. Transportation costs are incurred when shipping the product from the plant to satellite warehouses and from there to the final points of sale. The most important way to be competitive in this aspect of the industry is to carefully manage the utilization and maintenance of the fleet of delivery trucks. For example, whenever possible, bottlers try to get trucks returning to the plants from the warehouses and points of sale to carry back raw materials. Moreover, firms are constantly examining the trade-off between vehicle life and maintenance costs in order to optimize the use of their fleet.

Supermarkets are by far the most important channel for large-volume outlets in the soft drink industry (see Slide #5). In 1996, they accounted for 87% of the total distribution channel of packaged soft drinks (the other being mass merchandisers and drug stores). This fact is related to the packaging trend discussed above. Soft drink companies have found that the grocery store consumer usually buys about the same number of bottles or cartons of soft drink each week. Therefore, the more each package holds, the more product will be sold. This is an important reason why plastic bottles were introduced and promoted by the industry. Plastic is lighter than glass and enables companies to produce larger-sized bottles. The increased size of the package (the 2-liter plastic bottle being the most popular) holds more soft drink and of course generates more revenue and profit.

PRICING, ADVERTISING, AND PROMOTION

Because the soft drink industry is dominated by a few very large firms, its pricing structure is based on what economists refer to as "mutual interdependence." That is, each firm sets the price of its product with an explicit consideration of how the other firms will react. Therefore, prices are generally set by the industry leaders (i.e., Coca-Cola and Pepsi), and the other firms follow suit. Occasionally, the two giants have engaged in price wars with each other in an attempt to gain market share in different regions of the country.[3]

---

[3] For example, several years ago in an effort to penetrate the lucrative soft drink market in Texas, Pepsi initiated some very aggressive price discounting.

There is less market power (i.e., the power to set prices) in the market for the inputs which go into the making of soft drinks. Prices of such raw materials as sugar, high fructose corn syrup, aluminum, plastic, and glass are more subject to the volatility of supply and demand conditions. However, the two major companies exercise considerable bargaining power for the price at which they buy the raw materials, because they purchase these materials in such large quantities. Smaller multiple franchise bottlers and independents try to achieve economies in bulk purchases by forming cooperative arrangements with each other.

Because pricing is usually set and held at fairly similar levels by the major firms, competition among all the firms exists primarily in the area of advertising and promotion. Soft drink companies easily spend over $500 million just on television advertising. As you can easily imagine, the lion's share of this money was spent by the two giants. Promotions involve the sponsoring of major public events, discount pricing, and special packaging. For example, for its promotion during the 1988 holiday season, Coca-Cola offered its product in its old-fashioned Coke bottle. In 1992, it was a major sponsor of the Winter Olympics and in 1996 it was a major sponsor of the Summer Olympics.

NEW PRODUCTS

Since its beginning over 100 years ago, the soft drink industry has experimented with many different flavors. But perhaps the most important new products in its history have been the low-calorie drink and the decaffeinated drink. (Indeed, products are now available free of both sugar and caffeine.) Between 1981 and 1993, diet soft drinks rose from 14% of industry sales to 28.2%. Diet Coke had risen to become the third best-selling soft drink in the United States, with a phenomenal 8.6% share of the market in 1998 (see Slide #6). However, the market for diet soft drinks is shrinking from its peak of 29.8% in 1991. This saturated category continues to struggle due to intensified competition from new age products, although Diet Coke remains the number one brand.

A new addition to the soft drink industry included Slice, which was introduced in the mid-1980s by Pepsi-Cola. It is a citrus-based carbonated drink containing 10% fruit juice. Nevertheless, the product has not been very successful, representing less than one percent of the total soft drink market in 1998, and its market share continues to decline.

COMPETITION

Although the soft drink industry continues to grow in the United States, albeit more slowly than in the past, there is increasing competition from other non-alcoholic beverages. Bottled water continues to make inroads at 12.2% of the total beverage market (refer to Slide #1.) Per capita consumption of bottled water increased to 13.9 gallons in 1998—a 17% increase over 1997's level of 11.9 gallons. Retail dollar sales increased by 11% to $5.2 billion in 1998.

The second most popular non-alcoholic beverage in the U.S. in 1998 was fruit beverages (a category that includes both fruit juices and fruit-based drinks that are not 100% juice). According to *Beverage World*, fruit beverages accounted for $17.5 billion in retail sales for 1998, up 15% from 1997. The growth in this category is driven by consumers' growing awareness of health and nutrition. There still remains competition from ready-to-drink teas and sports drinks, yet per-capita consumption has remained constant over 1997 levels for these two product categories.

Since the soft drink industry is mature, growing at 2% to 3% per year, increased sales growth must come from international markets or the introduction of new products. Coca-Cola has the edge in the fast-growing international market, deriving close to 67% of its sales in 1998 from abroad. On the other hand, Pepsi-Cola's international sales decreased 9.7% in 1998, resulting in only 45% of total sales. Yet, Pepsi-Cola is ahead of Coca-Cola in the "alternative" drink market with non-alcoholic products such as Ocean Spray introduced in 1991, Lipton Iced Teas introduced in 1992, and AquaFina (bottled water) introduced in 1994.[4]

GOVERNMENTAL ISSUES

Interestingly enough, government regulation has been a factor to contend with, primarily in the use of the industry's new products. For example, in 1977 tests by the Food & Drug Administration indicated that acrylonitrile (the material used in the original plastic bottles) was a carcinogen. This caused Coca-Cola to suspend the use of this material in its bottling operations. Eventually, the entire industry shifted to the use of polyethylene terephthalate, a material with which the FDA apparently has no problem.

The other governmental decision which has had a major impact on the industry was the FDA's approval in 1982 for the use of aspartame as a sugar-substitute in diet soft drinks. This product is 200 times sweeter than sugar, although more costly than saccharin, the other commonly used non-sugar sweetener. By the latter half of the 1980s, virtually all diet soft drinks were sweetened by aspartame. The patent for aspartame, which was held by Monsanto, expired in December 1992. Since then, prices have fallen with increased competition from Holland Sweetener.

In 1998, the FDA approved two long-anticipated high-intensity sweeteners for the beverage industry: sucralose from McNeil Specialties, and acesulfame potassium from Nutrinova. A number of beverage companies have jumped in with new products using these sweeteners. Pepsi-Cola had the biggest new product offering with their new PepsiOne, which is made with a blend of acesulfame potassium (branded as Sunett) and aspartame. Coca-Cola decided to not introduce a new diet product with these new sweeteners, as the company is taking a wait-and-see approach with the new ingredients.

---

[4] *The Economist*, August 6, 1994, pp. 54-55, and PepsiCo, Inc. 1994 Annual Report.

Slide 1. U.S. Liquid Consumption Trends
Share of Beverage Gallonage in Percentage

	1997	1998
Soft Drinks	49.2%	49.0%
Beer	19.8%	19.4%
Fruit Beverages	13.4%	13.2%
Bottled Water	10.7%	12.2%
Sports Drinks	1.8%	1.8%
Wine	1.7%	1.7%
RTD Tea	2.3%	1.6%
Spirits	1.1%	1.1%

Source: 1998—*Beverage World*, May 1999, p.58.
1997—*S&P Industry Survey*, 11/26/98, p.12.

Slide 2. Franchise Leaders Market Share 1998

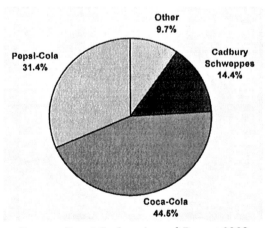

Source: *Pepsi Co Inc. Annual Report 1998.*

Slide 3. National Flavor Trends, 1993
Colas Continue to Dominate

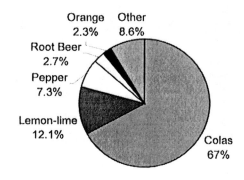

Source: *S&P Industry Surveys,* 8/18/94.

Slide 4. Packaging Mix 1998
Convenience is "King"

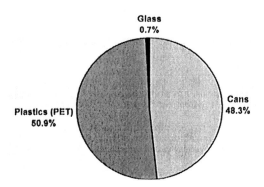

Source: *Beverage World,* June 1999, p.42.

Slide 5. Distribution by Large Volume Outlets 1996

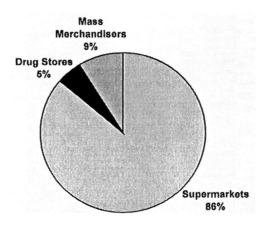

Source: *Beverage Industry Annual Manual 1997/98.*

Slide 6. Top 10 Soft Drinks 1998

Rank	Brand	Market Share %	'98 Growth
1	Coca-Cola Classic	20.6	+3.0%
2	Pepsi-Cola	14.5	+0.6%
3	Diet Coke	8.6	+4.0%
4	Mountain Dew	6.7	+11.0%
5	Sprite	6.5	+9.0%
6	Dr. Pepper	5.9	+5.8%
7	Diet Pepsi	5.0	+1.0%
8	7 UP	2.1	-2.7%
9	Caffeine Free Diet Coke	1.8	+4.0%
10	Minute Maid	1.2	+30.0%
	Other	27.0	+ 1.4%

Source: *Beverage World*, March 1999.

CHAPTER 1
INTRODUCTION

QUESTIONS

1.   Scarcity is a condition that exists when resources are limited relative to the demand for their use. Another way of describing this condition is to state that scarcity exists when resources are not available in unlimited amounts. When resources are available in unlimited amounts, economists consider them to be "free" goods. Because of the scarcity of resources, choices have to be made about their allocation among competing uses. Each choice is considered by economists to involve an "opportunity cost" because the use of scarce resources in one activity implies that they cannot be used in an alternative one. In other words, this opportunity cost is the amount that is sacrificed when choosing one activity over its next best alternative.

   It is reasonable to assume that all organizations have to work with scarce resources, no matter how large or profitable. A key role that managers play is to decide how best to allocate their organizations' scarce resources. From an economic standpoint, optimal decisions involve their weighing of the benefits associated with a particular decision against the opportunity cost of this decision.

2.   "What?"—This involves deciding what goods and services to produce and in what quantities (e.g., guns versus butter, capital goods versus consumer goods, etc.)

   "How?"—This involves deciding how best to allocate a country's resources in the production of particular goods or services (e.g., capital intensive versus labor intensive, domestic production versus foreign production etc.).

   "For whom?"—This involves deciding how to distribute a country's total output of goods and services (e.g., income and wealth distribution).

3.   a.   how
     b.   what
     c.   for whom
     d.   how
     e.   how

4.   Market Process: The use of supply, demand and material incentives (e.g., the profit motive) to decide how scarce resources are to be allocated. It answers the three questions of what, how and for whom in the following ways:

   "What?"—Whatever is profitable will be produced. Profitability in turn depends on the strength of a society's demand for a particular good or service and the cost to producers of providing such a good or service.

   "How?"—Resources should be allocated and combined in the least costly way.

   "For whom?"—The output of goods and services should be allocated to whomever is willing and able to pay for them. Of course the ability to pay depends on the country's distribution of income. Many factors may account for the distribution of income in a market economy. For economists, one of the most important is the "productivity principle." This states that income is allocated according to the relative productivity of the various factors of production.

5. As much as managers in a market economy rely on demand, cost, and profitability to guide them in their economic decisions, we have observed that command and tradition continue to play an important role in the decision-making process. In particular:

Command Process: Strategic, long-term or "political" decisions that are made by some central authority in an organization (in a large company it might be for example the CEO, the corporate management committee, in a small company it might be the owner/operator) can be considered part of the command process. For example, a manager might believe that a particular product is not profitable and recommend that it be dropped for the company's product line. However, upper management might believe that the product might have some long-term or strategic value and override this decision. The opposite might also be true.

A good example of this is the case of the IBM typewriter. In 1984, IBM made a major strategic decision to stay in the business of making typewriters, even though analysis indicated that it would become increasingly more difficult for it to be profitable in this business as typewriters became electronic rather that electromechanical and as PCs and word processors performed more and more of the basic typing functions. It invested approximately $500 million to completely modernize and automate its production facilities in Lexington, Kentucky. A major reason for maintaining and investing further in this business was because upper management believed that for strategic reasons, IBM needed to have its own capability of making keyboards for its computers.

In 1990, IBM decided to spin off its typewriter division to a separate, privately owned company called Lexmark. (We do not know whether it was because the typewriter division was not profitable.)

Of course, managers in a market economy must also deal with the command process whenever government rules, regulations, or laws have to be considered. Chapter 15 of this text is devoted to this possibility.

Traditional Process: As pointed out in the text, customs and traditions play a more important role for managers in developing countries. However, we have observed or read about certain instances in which they affect management decisions here in the United States. For example, some years back it was reported in the Wall Street Journal that the CEO of International Harvester (now operating as Navistar) lamented that the company should have sold off its farm equipment long before it actually did. However, he pointed out that he and the rest of the management found it very difficult to divest itself of the product line on which the company was founded.

If the instructor wishes, he or she may wish to bring up the whole issue of the traditional view of occupations for men and women. For example, years ago, suitable professional work for women was usually confined to teaching and nursing. Obviously, this traditional view of the role of women in the workplace has changed in the United States. However, in the rest of the world, even in the developed countries such as Japan and those in Western Europe, tradition is still an important factor.

Instructors may also wish to consider the traditional view and acceptance of various unethical practices such as kick-backs in government contracts and the practice of nepotism in the hiring of personnel that exists today in many developing countries.

6. This question is subject to considerable interpretation and the instructor may choose to use his or her own distinctions between the two concepts. We believe that management skills have to do more with the organizing and management of scarce resources (particular the managing of people) and entrepreneurship has more to do with the taking of certain risks in such activities as the introduction of goods and services to the marketplace. Ideally, the successful manager or entrepreneur should have both capabilities.

7. Microeconomics focuses on individual markets for goods and services, while macroeconomics focuses on aggregate economic activity. Managers should understand the macroeconomy in order to prepare for or operate more effectively over different phases of the business cycle. For example, if managers believe that the economy will soon come out of a recession, they may want to begin building inventories or making certain capital investments in order to better handle the increased demand which accompanies a recovery. Or managers may want to consider diversifying their firm's portfolio of goods and services to include some products that are "recession proof" (i.e., those with income elasticities that are very low or negative).

8. Marketing is the key to success in this industry. Specifically, this includes all of the "four P's of marketing": pricing, product, promotion, and placement. Production is also important. Recently, PepsiCo has been buying a selected number of independently owned bottlers because it believes it can operate them more efficiently and also gain certain economies of scale.

   Our background paper on this industry should give instructors further information to discuss this question with the class.

9. Note to Instructors: Here are some suggested answers. These may be modified depending on changing events.

   a. Telecommunications: This is a rapidly changing industry for all types of companies. Let us suggest an answer for the regional bell operating companies or the RBOCs.

      Competition: Certain states like California are already allowing other companies such as AT&T and MCI to offer competing local service.

      Technology: Wireless communications in the form of cellular phone service is rapidly growing. Personal communications service (PCS) could well be another competing type of wireless competition.

   b. Retail Merchandising:

      Competition: "Category busters" such as Home Depot, Sports Authority, and Borders Books have become real threats to the existence of smaller retail stores. Everyday low price (EDLP) stores such as Wal-Mart and K-Mart continue to grow and dominate the retail scene.

      Technology: Large chains such as Wal-Mart are able to send sales data on a daily basis back to headquarters, enabling financial analysts to track closely inventory and product category sales.

   c. Higher Education: The Internet has enabled institutions to offer online, distance learning classes. It is now possible to obtain a degree without attending any classes on a "physical" campus. The "virtual" campus is now a reality.

d.   Aerospace and Defense:

Customers: The federal government, the major customer for aerospace and defense companies, has been cutting back its spending in the post-cold-war era.

CHAPTER 2
THE FIRM AND ITS GOALS

QUESTIONS

1. Yes. The company can profit from this action in several ways. Graduate students, impressed with the computers, may become recruits for the computer firm. This increases the employment market for the firm, and it may become able to hire some superior graduates. Or, these students, after graduation, will work for other firms and recommend the computer made by this manufacturer for use in their work place. In short, if the additional profits from future sales exceed the cost of the donation, then such a policy is quite consistent with profit maximization.

2. This is an incomplete objective, and may not be consistent with the objective of profit maximization. Setting a profit margin too high may result in smaller profits than could possibly be achieved with a lower profit margin. In other words, setting a profit margin may not result in profit maximization.

3. This comment is incorrect. It is quite true that the existence of consumer organizations, legal requirements and warranty requirements may raise a company's costs above what they would have been in their absence. But such costs will now be included in a company's cost calculations. Given these costs, a company can still attempt to maximize its profits under the new circumstances. The total profit level will be lower than if these costs did not exist, but the process of profit maximization will still be in place.

4. Shareholder wealth maximization is the more comprehensive of the two. Profit maximization is a period of value that may be obtained by short-term management action which could be detrimental to profits in future periods.

    But a company with longer range horizons will want to consider a stream of earnings (or cash flows) over time. This stream is then discounted at the company's cost of capital to the present to obtain the present value of this stream. This present value is the value of the firm or that of the stockholders. When such an objective is used, the company is considering the shape and duration of the cash flow stream and the return required by stockholders (i.e. the equity cost of capital). The required rate of return is affected by risk, and, thus, risk enters into the valuation. Obviously, this measure is much more inclusive than the maximization of profit for any one period.

5. Stockholders generally may not know what maximum profits their firm could generate. Thus, they will look for a satisfactory return (both dividend and price appreciation). Company management will not be held to maximization but will manage the corporation in a way as to satisfy the shareholders. The term often used to describe this is "satisficing."

6. Since the ownership in a corporation is widely dispersed, and thus individual stockholders have little power, it may be believed by managers that it is not necessary to endeavor to maximize company profits. Since the managers usually own only a small fraction of the corporation's stock, their interest may not be served best by maximizing the value of the corporation. Thus they may be more interested in maximizing their own incomes and perquisites. They may also not take prudent risks to maximize returns, since a severe reversal in business fortunes could cause them to lose their positions. Not taking the appropriate risks may result in rather mediocre but still satisfactory shareholder returns.

7. There are several forces which will tend to create a convergence between the interests of stockholders and managers, and thus cause managers to be interested in maximizing a corporation's profits or value:

    a. Corporate shares are not only owned by widely dispersed stockholders but by large institutional holders (banks, insurance companies, mutual funds, pension funds). These organizations employ analysts who continually study stock performance. Non-performing companies would be sold from these institutions' portfolios, and lead to decreased prices of these stocks. This could then result in takeovers by other companies, proxy fights, etc. which could lead to the dismissal of present management.

    b. Competitive pressures could lead to stock price declines for a non-performing company, and again result in takeovers, proxy contests, etc.

    c. In many corporations, management remuneration is tied to performance and managers frequently are awarded stock options which gain value as the price of shares rises. Thus, managers will have an interest in maximizing stockholder welfare.

8. It probably does. Other types of objectives may be partial; but profit and wealth maximization still appear to be the most inclusive objectives. Further, it is much more possible to test this hypothesis than some of the others.

9. No. Accounting depreciation is calculated on historical costs. Thus, depreciating a machine which cost $10,000 when originally purchased can result only in a maximum of $10,000 of depreciation charges set aside toward the purchase of a replacement machine. If this machine (due to inflation) now costs $20,000, then the funds earmarked for the new machine will be insufficient to purchase it. For economists, replacement costs are the relevant quantities.

10. Implicit costs can include in them costs not considered by accountants, such as the owners' opportunity costs. Thus, accounting profit would generally be higher than economic profit. Economists would include opportunity costs in their calculation of costs; economists' costs include what is usually referred to as normal profit.

11. You would compare the amount of time spent on each employment, the interest that you could earn on your investment in your business against keeping your funds invested elsewhere (i.e. savings account or other), and the risk involved in the two alternatives. You may even include some estimate (hard to quantify) of any psychic value you derive from being your own boss.

12. Depreciation should reflect the actual change in the value of the equipment and the change in the equipment's replacement cost.

13. A multinational corporation is usually faced with different legal, economic, cultural and tax conditions in the many countries in which it operates. Such considerations will complicate greatly the tasks of a corporation's managers and create constraints on their actions. However, if management learns to live with such additional risk and restrictions, corporations can still pursue the goal of profit maximization.

14. A firm will seek to carry out its operations at minimum cost. Until recently, operations such as cafeteria, copying, etc., had to be operated by the company itself, since there were no specialized companies offering such services. However, as the demand for such services has risen, businesses

specializing in these endeavors were organized, serving a large number of companies requiring them. Because of this demand, these new businesses can achieve a size where they can supply these services more cheaply than the individual firms can. The cost of contracting this activity to the outside has become lower than organizing it internally.

15.   High transaction costs will cause a firm to internalize some of its costs. Some of the reasons for high transaction costs are:

    a.   The negotiation and enforcement of contracts.
    b.   Uncertainty and frequency of transactions.
    c.   Assets-specificity which may lead to opportunistic behavior.

16.   Using the constant dividend growth formula $P = D_1/(k - g)$:
      $2 \times 1.06/(.13 - .06) = 2.12/.07 = \$30.29$ per share
      $30.29 \times 2,000,000 = \$60.6$ million

17.   Shareholder wealth is calculated by multiplying the number of shares outstanding by the price of the stock. MVA is the difference between the market value of the company (including both stocks and bonds) and the capital contributed by the investors. The latter concept is more meaningful since it measures the increase in wealth of the investors above what they have contributed. A company could have a very high market value, but investors may have actually contributed more than the company is worth. In such a case, there has been a destruction of investors' value. General Motors appears to be an example of such a situation.

CHAPTER 2A
APPENDIX

QUESTIONS

1. Function: The relationship between a dependent variable and one (or more) independent variables.

    Variable: An entity that can assume different values

    Independent Variable: Variable whose value is determined independently of the value of any other variable being considered in a functional relationship.

    Dependent Variable: Variable whose value depends on the value of some other (independent) variable.

    Functional Form: The particular way in which the value of a dependent variable is affected by the value of one or more independent variables.

2. Assume the following demand equation: $Q_D = 250 - 10P$. Given this linear equation, we can express demand tabular form as follows:

P	Q
$25	0
20	50
15	100
10	150
5	200
0	250

    We can also plot this on a graph with P on the vertical axis (as is usually done in economics) or on the horizontal axis (as would be the case according to mathematical convention).

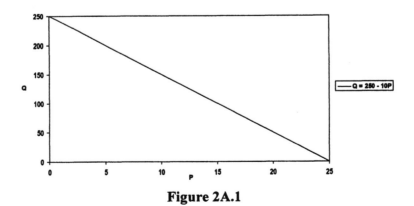

Figure 2A.1

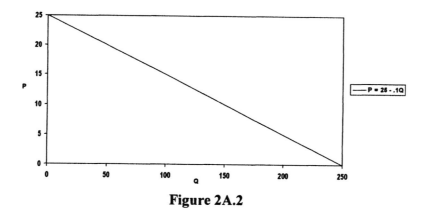

Figure 2A.2

3. The following are suggested ways to answer this question. Instructors may wish to devise their own equations.

    a. $Q_D = f(A)$ where A = dollar amount spent on advertising

    b. Q = f(L) where Q = units of output and L = number of labor hours employed in the production process

    c. Q/L = f(K) where Q/L units of output per labor hour and K = units of machinery (or dollar value of machinery) used in the production process

    d. TR = f(P), II = f(P) where TR = total revenue, II = total profit and P = price

    e. TR = f(Y), II = f(Y) where Y= real GNP

    f. TR = f(D), II = f(D) where D = Dow-Jones Industrial Average

    g. TVC = f(PER) where TVC = total variable cost and PER = percentage of dollar value of components manufactured by outside vendors.

4. A function is said to be continuous over a given interval if it is continuous <u>at every point</u> on that interval. In real world situations, it may be impractical to consider the value of an economic variable at every point on the interval. For example, the price of a product might be considered in intervals of $1, $10 or even larger. Thus to consider one cent (and even smaller points in an interval) would simply be impractical. Nonetheless, the assumption of continuity does not negate the basic functional relationships among economic variables and in fact enables us to use calculus to analyze these relationships.

5. The slope of a line measures the rate of change of the dependent variable with respect to some independent variable. It is important because much of economic analysis is based on the incremental or marginal analysis of designated variables. (See the answer to question 6 for an elaboration of this point.)

6. Marginal analysis is the consideration of small changes around some given point. If discrete changes are considered then a unit change is usually considered. (e.g., marginal revenue is equal to the change in total revenue relative to a unit change in quantity). Sometimes, it may not be practical or desirable to consider unit changes in the independent variable. Instead, a manager may wish to

consider the change in revenue resulting from the introduction of a new project in a given time period. For example, the managers of Global Foods might want consider the additional annual revenue resulting from its entry into the soft drink market rather than the annual revenue associated with each additional can of product sold. If this is the case, then we can say that "incremental analysis" is being used. Both marginal and incremental analysis are similar because both consider changes in variables instead of their total values.

7. The first derivative of a function is important because it determines the rate of change of a dependent variable with respect to an independent variable. Economists are generally interested in the impact that an independent variable has on the designated dependent variable.

8. By setting the first derivative equal to zero and solving for the value of the independent variable that satisfies this condition, we arrive at the maximum or the minimum value of the dependent variable.

9. An analysis of the second derivative of a function enables us to distinguish between a function's maximum and minimum value, in the event that it has both. If at the point where the first derivative is zero we find the second derivative to be positive, then we know that the function is minimized; if the second derivative is negative, then we know that the function is maximized.

10. $\Delta Y / \Delta X$ indicates discrete changes in Y relative to X. dY/dX indicates the change in Y relative to a very small (i.e., infinitesimally small) change in X. Both give the same answer if the function is linear.

PROBLEMS

1.   a.   Q = 75 - .5P

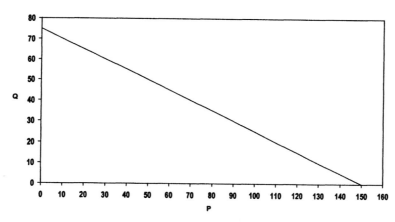

Figure 2A.3

b.   P = 150 -2Q

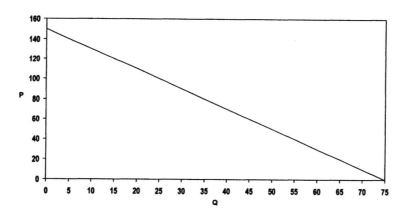

Figure 2A.4

2.   (a, b, and c are answered together for each equation)

$Q = 450 - 16P$
$P = 28.125 - .0625Q$
$TR = 28.125Q - .0625Q^2$
$MR = 28.125 - .125Q$
$Q^* = 225$
$P^* = \$14.06$

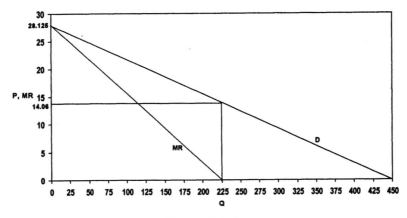

Figure 2A.5

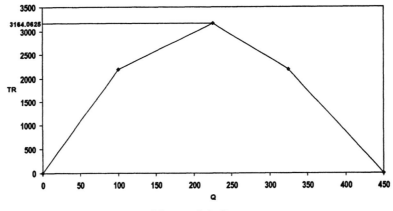

Figure 2A.6

Q = 360 - 80P
P = 4.5 - .0125Q
TR = 4.5Q - .0125Q²
MR = 4.5 - .025Q²
Q* = 180
P* = $2.25

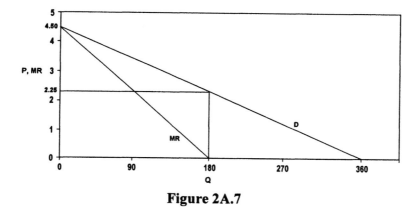

Figure 2A.7

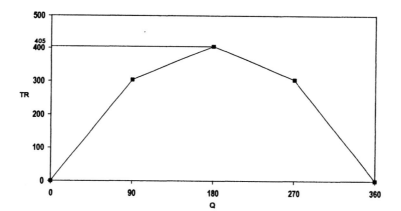

Figure 2A.8

Q = 1500 - 500P
P = 3 - .002Q
TR = 3Q - .002Q²
MR = 3 - .004Q
Q* = 750
P* = $1.50

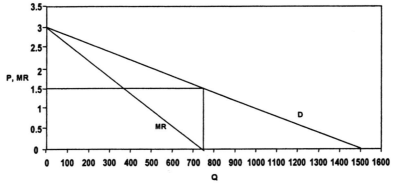

Figure 2A.9

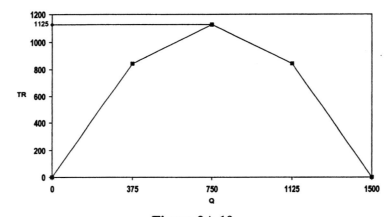

Figure 2A.10

3.   a.

$$TC = 1500 + 300Q - 25Q^2 + 1.5Q^3$$
$$AC = \frac{1500}{Q} + 300 - 25Q + 1.5Q^2$$
$$AVC = 300 - 25Q + 1.5Q^2$$
$$MC = 300 - 50Q + 4.5Q^2$$

$$TC = 1500 + 300Q + 25Q^2$$
$$AC = \frac{1500}{Q} + 300 + 25Q^2$$
$$AVC = 300 + 25Q$$
$$MC = 300 + 50Q$$

$$TC = 1500 + 300Q$$
$$AC = \frac{1500}{Q} + 300$$
$$AVC = 300$$
$$MC = 300$$

b.   For graphs of these equations, please refer to the next page.

c.   In order to determine the quantity that minimizes the marginal cost in the cubic equation, take the derivative of the marginal cost function, set equal to zero, and then solve for Q.

For the first of the equations, the answer is $Q^* = 5.5$. As can be seen from the graphs, the marginal costs in the second and third equations have no minimum points.

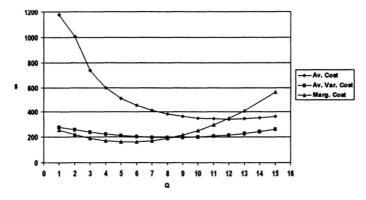

Figure 2A.11

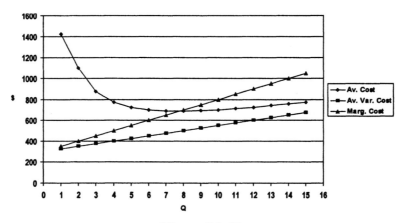

Figure 2A.12

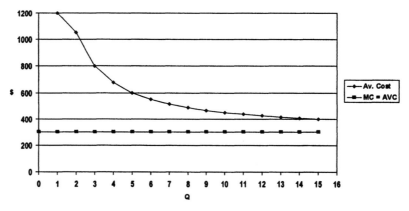

Figure 2A.13

4.   Problems a. and b. are answered together for each equation.

$Q = 10 - .004P$
$P = 2500 - 250Q$
$TR = 2500Q - 250Q^2$
$MR = 2500 - 500Q$

For the first (cubic) equation, setting MR=MC and solving for Q:

$-4.5Q^2 - 450Q + 2200 = 0$

$$Q^* = -104.6 \text{ or } 4.67$$
$$= 4.67$$
$$P^* = \$1332.50$$

For the second (quadratic) equation, setting MR=MC and solving for Q:

$5500Q = 2200$
$Q^* = 4$
$P^* = \$1500$

For the third (linear) equation, setting MR=MC and solving for Q:

$500Q = 2200$
$Q^* = 4.4$
$P^* = \$1400$

The graphs of the profit functions for each of these examples are shown below and on the next page.

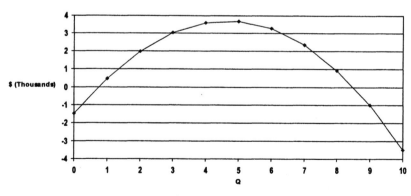

Figure 2A.14

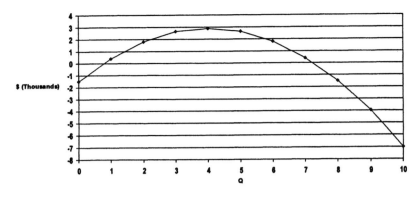

Figure 2A.15

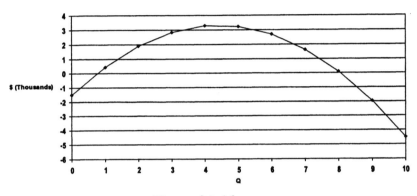

Figure 2A.16

CHAPTER 3
SUPPLY AND DEMAND

QUESTIONS

1. Demand: Quantities of a good or service that people are ready to buy at different prices, other factors held constant.

    Supply: Quantities of a good or service that people are ready to sell at different prices, other factors held constant.

    "Demand" encompasses all possible quantities demanded at different prices, while "quantity demanded" refers to one particular amount that people are ready to buy out of the entire set of possibilities. The former is represented by the entire demand curve; the latter is represented by a point on the curve.

    A similar distinction can be made about "supply" and "quantity supplied."

2. Demand: 1) income; 2) tastes and preferences; 3) prices of related products; 4) future expectations; 5) number of buyers

    Supply: 1) costs; 2) technology; 3) prices of other products sold by suppliers; 4) future expectations; 5) number of sellers; 6) weather conditions

3. An important part of the functioning of the market process is the determination of the price of a particular product as well as the relative prices of all goods and services in the market. As we have shown in this chapter, it is the price that serves as the rationing agent in the short run whenever the market is not in equilibrium (i.e., shortages or surpluses exist). It is also the price that serves as a "signal" in the long run to buyers and sellers concerning what markets to focus their purchases and production efforts.

4. Comparative statics analysis is an approach to studying a problem that is frequently used in economics. In the analysis of the market process, it begins by stating certain assumptions about market conditions and then establishing equilibrium price and quantity. One (or more) of the assumptions are changed, creating a disequilibrium in the market. As a result, new equilibrium price and output levels are then determined. The new equilibrium levels are then compared to the original ones.

5. This function involves the increase or decrease in price to clear the market of any shortage or surplus. It is considered a function that takes effect in the short run market time period. If the price did not change accordingly, buyers would face long lines, waiting lists, and other inconvenient manifestations of a market shortage. Sellers would be left with unwanted inventories of goods.

6. This function takes effect in the long run market time period. Resources are guided into or out of markets as a result of increases or decreases in the price.

7. Short Run, Producers' Perspective: Time enough only to react to changes in demand (and price) by changing their variable factors of production.

Long Run, Producers' Perspective: Time enough to react to changes in demand (and price) by changes all factors of production.

Short Run, Consumers' Perspective: Time enough to react to changes in supply (and price) by changing the quantity demanded. (For example, if the price of gasoline rises, people will react in the short run simply by buying less at the higher price.)

Long Run, Consumers' Perspective: Time enough to react to changes in supply (and price) by changing demand. (For example, if the price of gasoline rises, people will react in the long run by car pooling, buying more fuel efficient cars, and changing their patterns of automobile usage, thus causing demand for gasoline to shift to the left.)

8. From an economic standpoint, a shortage exists when the quantity demanded exceeds the quantity supplied at some given price. In other words, it exists because the price is too low relative to its market clearing or equilibrium point.

    Scarcity is a relative situation reflected in the market equilibrium price. For example, if the price of a particular good rises, then we can say that in economic terms, it has now become scarcer. If the price of a particular good is higher than another one, then we can say that the former is scarcer than the latter.

    We can use the contrast between the short run and long run market time periods (along with comparative statics analysis) to illustrate the difference between a shortage and a surplus. Let us assume that we are analyzing the market for oranges.

    * Late frost destroys a sizable proportion of the Florida orange crop. Supply for oranges shifts to the left.

    * As a result in the decrease in supply, a <u>shortage</u> is created at the existing market price for oranges.

    * Because of the shortage, the price of oranges rises.

    * This rise in the equilibrium price of oranges indicates to market participants that oranges are<u>more scarce.</u>

    * In the long run, demand for oranges may begin to decrease as the price signal indicating that they are more scarce causes people to economize on the consumption of this commodity.

9. It is important because it will help them to analyze what might be currently happening as well as what <u>might</u> happen in a particular market.

    For example, suppose the managers of a firm that produces bottled water experience an unexpected increase in the demand for their product because of changing consumer tastes and preferences and the increasing concern over the purity of available tap water. Simply enjoying the benefits of this rise in demand will not be advisable, because they should realize that over time (i.e., in the "long run") many new companies will seek to enter the now more lucrative bottled water market. (In the U.S. Perrier has met with considerable competition from Evian and others. To be sure, their sales were hurt because of quality control problems. However, a point can be made that because of the increase in competition which inevitably faces successful companies in the long run, it should have been even more careful to control the purity of its product.)

10.   We can use the actual example of the additional tax of 10 percent levied on luxury cars sold for over $30,000. This tax certainly increases the actual price of the car to the consumer. Assuming a normal downward sloping demand curve, less cars will be demanded (i.e., there will be a movement along the demand curve for luxury cars). However, it is not certain whether the price will actually fall in the long run. Over time, the demand for luxury cars might shift to the left but then again it might not. This is because in reality, all "other factors" do not remain constant. For example, tastes and preferences may change in favor of luxury cars or the economy may experience a strong recovery and expansion.

In addition, the market for luxury cars might not be perfectly competitive. In other words, to keep the price of cars from falling, the manufacturers might scale back production, (thereby causing the supply of luxury cars to shift to the left.)

11.   Economists make the distinction between "demand" and "quantity demanded" in order to facilitate the use of the supply and demand diagrams in explaining the rationing and guiding functions of price. However, in the business world, this distinction is usually not made. For business people, the term "demand" is generally used in reference to both "demand" and "quantity demanded." Whether the former or the latter term is being considered depends on the context in which they are used. In the above statement, "demand" clearly refers to the economist's "quantity demanded."

As instructors, we have noticed that economics texts books (particularly principles texts) greatly stress the difference between these two terms, and rightfully so. However, this question is to remind students that in applying demand analysis to actual situations, business people usually ignore this distinction.

12.   a.   Busier life styles, two-income families, single-parent households will continue to cause demand for convenience foods to increase.

b.   Demand is already increasing drastically for goods purchased on the Internet and is posed to explode in the next five years.

c.   Will decline as usage of internal fax modems and e-mail attachments continue to rise.

d.   May decrease as digital cameras become less expensive and in greater demand.

e.   Pay-per-view and satellite TV programs will continue to erode video rental demand.

f.   Pay-per-view should increase as broader band connections to the home make this form of entertainment cheaper and easier to use.

g.   Longer term trends point in an upward direction.

h.   It is difficult to tell, but if demand for SUV's and trucks continues to rise, there will also be a steady increase in demand (particularly in the U.S. and Western Europe). Also, if emerging markets continue to grow (particularly in countries such as China and Brazil), there will be more automobiles and hence an increase in world demand for gasoline.

13.   a.   (1) Discovery of new sources of oil: supply increases. (2) Invention of new long-lasting battery for electric car: supply decreases—particularly in the long run as companies shift their resources from oil production to battery production. (3) Mergers or acquisitions (as have been going on in the late 90s with BP and Amoco as well as Exxon and Mobil):—these mergers may

cause supply to increase or decrease depending on the intentions of the larger companies that have even more power over supply.

b. (1) Cattle ranching declines as it becomes harder to earn a good return in the market for beef (in this case it is actually supply decreasing in response to demand falling in the long run. (2) Increase in beef imports from countries such as Argentina (recently the U.S. government allowed the importation of Argentine beef into the country) —supply increases.

c. Increase in the building of new manufacturing facilities in Asian countries such as Taiwan—supply increases.

d. Mergers and acquisitions in the hotel industry (could increase or decrease number of rooms—would probably increase number of rooms as the larger companies try to expand their market share by building new hotels).

e. U.S. or European based multinationals such as McDonald's and Burger King build new restaurants in an attempt to expand their global businesses—supply increases.

f. New co-branded cards are offered by financial institutions—supply increases.

g. More manufacturing, assembly and distribution capacity by key companies such as Dell, Compaq, IBM and Gateway 2000—supply increases.

h. More PC companies such as Dell and Compaq 2000 enter the server market or increase their resources in this product segment in an attempt to offset the shrinking profit margins in the PC business --supply increases.

PROBLEMS

1.   a.   800 caps
       b. $10
       c. $20
       d.   Note to Instructors: If you assign this question, be sure to point out to your students that the answer is covered in Appendix 2A. It is also discussed in greater detail in Chapter 4. We ask this question simply as a prelude to the material in Chapter 4.

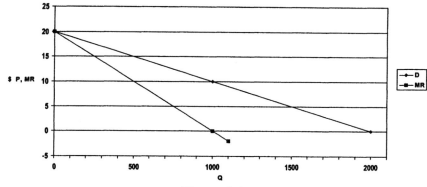

Figure 3.1

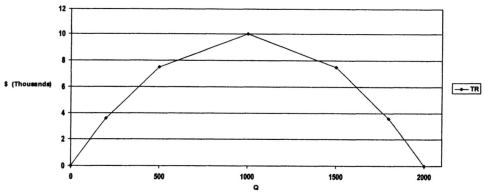

Figure 3.2

2.   a.

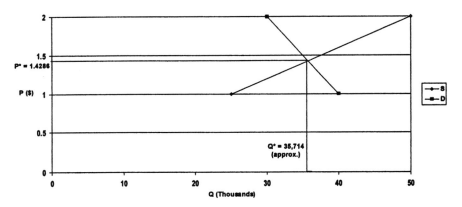

Figure 3.3

b. $25,000P = 50,000 - 10,000P$ $Q_d = 50,000 - 10,000 (1.4286) = 35,714$
      $35,000P = 50,000$ $Q_s = 25,000 (1.4286) = 35,714$
      $P^* = \$1.4286$

3.   a.

Price	Q_S	Q_D	Surplus or Shortage
$6.00	55,000	5,000	50,000
5.00	40,000	15,000	25,000
4.00	25,000	25,000	0
3.00	10,000	35,000	-25,000
2.00	0	45,000	-45,000
1.00	0	55,000	-55,000

b.   Equilibrium price = $4.00 because it equates Q_D with Q_S.

4.   a. $300
      b. $100
      c.

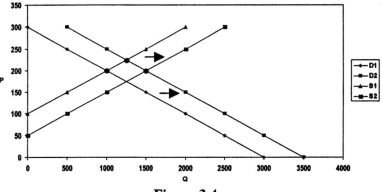

Figure 3.4

d. $P^* = \$200 \; Q^* = 1000$
e. $P^* = \$225 \; Q^* = 1250$
f. $P^* = \$200 \; Q^* = 1500$
g.   See graph above

5. a. $Q = 10,000 - 200P + .03(1,000,000) + .6(30,000) + .2(15,000)$

    $Q_D = 61,000 - 200P$

    b.

P	Q_D
$200	000
175	26,000
150	31,000
125	36,000

    c. $P = \$80$.

6. a. $Q = 200 - 300(2.50) + 120(10) + 65(60) - 250(15) + 400(10)$

    $Q = 200 - 750 + 1200 + 3900 - 3750 + 4000$

    $Q^* = 4800$

    $Q_D = 5550 - 300P$

    b. $Q_D = 3550$, a reduction of 1250 (or 5 X 250)

    c. Advertising expenditure would have to increase by 3.125 or $3,125 (i.e., 400 x 3.125 = 1250))

7. Supply curve shifts to right and demand curve shifts to left. The combined shifts drastically reduced the world market price for sugar.

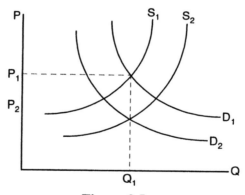

Figure 3.5

8. The main cause for the increase in the demand for CDs is the decrease in the price of CD players, the complementary product. Other factors might be the change in tastes and preferences in favor of CDs (favored for their durability, convenience, and clarity of sound), and the increase in income, particularly doing the booming second half of the 1980s.

    Although the demand for CDs has increased, the supply of CDs has probably increased more than the demand. Over the long run, new sellers enter, the production capacity of CD producers increase, the number of artists and CD titles increase, etc. See the diagrams on the following pages.

9.   (To Instructor: This problem is a precursor to the discussion of the elasticity concept, and could be discussed in conjunction with Chapter 4.)

   a. No, because point elasticity is -0.625.

   b. Yes. Although the number of units sold would drop from 12,000 to 10,000, the combined impact of an inelastic demand and the increase in advertising would raise total revenue from $36,000 to $40,000. Moreover, the incremental revenue is far greater than the $100 increase in advertising expenses.

10.   a. Q = 1,500 – 4(400) + 25(20) +10(15) + 3(500)
          = 2,050

   b. Advertising would have to increase by $12,000 in order for the firm to regain the loss of 300 units resulting from its competitor's reduction in price of $100.

   c. The price of substitute products such as cruise packages.

   d. If time series data were collected on a quarterly basis, then seasonal factors such as summer or winter could be introduced in the form of dummy variables.

11.   a. Q = 250 - 10P can be transformed into:
          P = 25 - .1Q

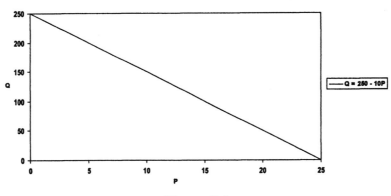

Figure 3.6

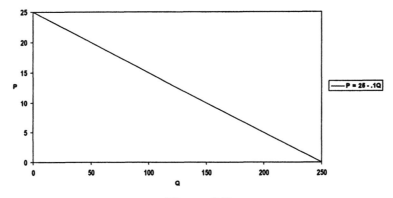

Figure 3.7

b. Q = 1300 - 140P can be transformed into:
   P = 9.29 - .007Q

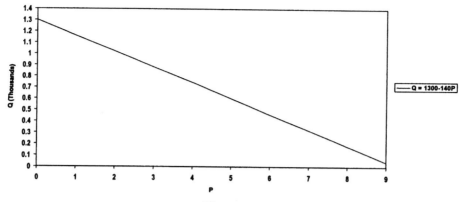

Figure 3.8

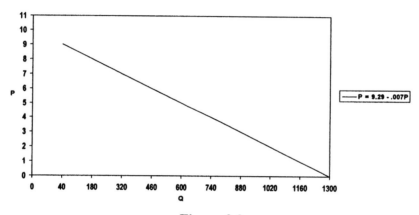

Figure 3.9

c. Q = 45 - .5P can be transformed into:
    P = 90 - 2Q

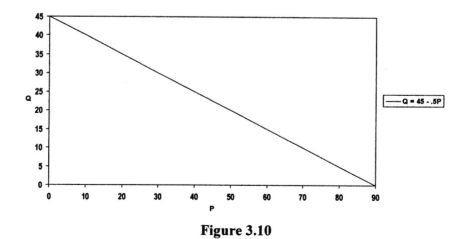

Figure 3.10

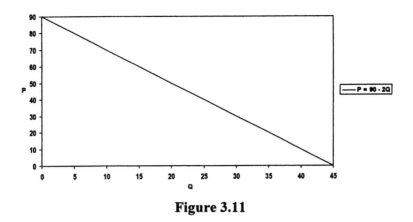

Figure 3.11

12.

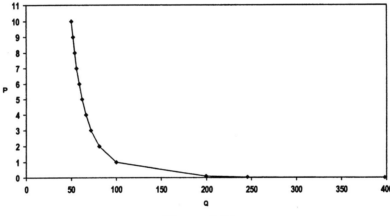

Figure 3.12

Certain consumer electronics products could exhibit this type of demand. This curve indicates that once the price falls to a threshold, the quantity demanded starts to "take off." Hand-held calculators, compact disk players, and perhaps even home computers could very well fit this situation.

CHAPTER 4
DEMAND ELASTICITY

QUESTIONS

1. Elasticity refers to the percentage change in one variable relative to a percentage change in another variable.

   Price elasticity of demand is defined as the percentage change in quantity resulting from a one percent change in price.

2. Point elasticity (in connection with the price elasticity of demand) refers to the elasticity at a given point on a demand curve. It measures the percentage change in quantity caused by a very small (actually infinitesimally small) percentage change in price. Arc elasticity measures the elasticity over a certain discrete segment of the demand curve.

   If arc elasticity were defined as

$$\frac{\text{change in quantity/quantity}}{\text{change in price/price}}$$

   then the elasticity coefficient would differ if we moved up on a demand curve as against moving down on it.

   To make an upward movement have the same elasticity coefficient as a movement down, average quantity and average price are used in the formula.

   In practical business situations, arc elasticity would probably be the more useful concept, because a businessperson would most likely be interested in the effect on quantity of a change in price of some discrete magnitude rather than an infinitesimally small change in price.

3. This result follows from an application of the notion of elasticity of derived demand. The demand for skilled crafts people is probably more inelastic than the demand for industrial workers. Thus a substantial increase in the wage of skilled crafts people would cause a smaller decrease in employment than a similar percentage increase in the wages of less skilled workers.

4. a. Probably fairly inelastic since mayonnaise is a staple and accounts for a small portion of a person's or a family's total budget.
    b. Probably fairly elastic, since there are many good substitutes for a specific brand of mayonnaise.
    c. Probably relatively elastic since there are numerous substitutes. Also, it represents a relatively large portion of a person's budget.
    d. As a "luxury," the demand elasticity for a Jaguar could be considered to be relatively elastic. But since such automobiles are purchased by people in a high income category, the demand elasticity could also be quite low. The answer probably depends on whether other high-priced cars (Mercedes, BMW, Infinity, etc.) are considered to be close substitutes.
    e. Probably rather elastic. It represents a significant expenditure. Further, a repair may significantly prolong its life.

    f. Probably rather elastic since other vacation arrangements (driving, bus, train) could be substituted. Also, it represents a significant portion of total vacation cost.

    g. Quite inelastic, since it is considered a staple, and usually represents a small part of a person's budget.

    h. Probably quite elastic since they represent a large expenditure. If given as a gift, there are probably many good substitutes.

5.   The income elasticity for restaurant food is probably quite high. Thus, during declines in economic activity (and thus, possibly declines in incomes), spending on restaurant food would most likely decline more than spending at home. Actually, since the two are substitutes, spending on food at home may actually go up during economic declines.

6.   a. Negative they are complements.

    b. Positive—they are substitutes.

    c. Positive—they are substitutes.

    d. Do not know—there is no relationship between these two products. However, both of these may compete for budget dollars. From a total budget viewpoint, they could be considered to be substitutes. But usually, the relationship between the two would be very tenuous.

7.   When the demand curve is inelastic, marginal revenue is negative. Thus, selling on the inelastic portion of the demand curve would result in a decrease in total revenue for every additional unit sold.

8.   Most likely automobiles, since they represent a larger expenditure.

9.   Yes. Elasticity of demand is expected to be higher in the long run. Thus, a larger decrease in gasoline consumption would have been expected. In fact, gasoline prices decreased to pre-crisis levels rather quickly.

10.   A five-cent increase probably did not affect consumption of gasoline significantly since it was a relatively small change. The demand for gasoline is probably relatively inelastic in such a small range. This is quite different from the doubling of prices which had occurred during the oil embargo in 1973, for instance.

11.   Since the demand curve for cigarettes and alcohol is generally thought to be rather inelastic, imposing a tax on these products would not be expected to decrease consumption a great deal. The tax revenue from such products would be considerably larger than from products whose demand curve was rather elastic and whose consumption would decrease greatly upon the imposition of an additional tax.

12.   No. Since the percentage changes between quantity and price are different at each point of the demand curve.

13.   This firm is faced by considerable competition. Theoretically, if it raises its price by any small amount, it would lose all of its business, because there are many other firms in the industry which are offering this same product at the lower price.

14.   False. If a company's demand curve is elastic, a price decrease will increase its revenue. But if, as it sells more, its costs should rise more than its revenue, the price action would decrease the company's profit. So, if the company wants to maximize its profits, it will not lower its price in this case.

15. a. Less than 1. Elasticity may actually be negative if consumers switch to more expensive butter as their incomes increase.

   b. Most likely greater than 1. This is a luxury item and increased income may bring about a larger than proportional increase in consumption.

   c. Probably close to 1. But, as incomes increase, consumers may switch to more expensive furniture. Thus elasticity could be greater than 1.

   d. Probably greater than 1. Since lobsters are generally an expensive food, people with increasing incomes may increase their expenditure on lobster more than proportionally.

16. A one percent increase in income will bring about a .25% increase in spending on tomatoes.

PROBLEMS

1. $$\frac{\% \text{ change } Q}{\% \text{ change } P} = \frac{.2}{-.1} = -2$$

2. a. $Q = 20 - 2P$; slope $\Delta Q/\Delta P = -2$

    At $P = 5$ $Q = 20 - 2 \times 5 = 10$
    At $P = 9$ $Q = 20 - 2 \times 9 = 2$

    When $Q = 10$ and $P = 5$ $\varepsilon_p = -2 \times 5/10 = -1$ Unitary elastic
    When $Q = 2$ and $P = 9$ $\varepsilon_p = -2 \times 9/2 = -9$ Elastic

    b. At $P = 5$, $Q = 10$
    At $P = 6$, $Q = 8$

    $$\begin{aligned} E_p &= (10 - 8)/(10 + 8) \div (5 - 6)/(5 + 6) \\ &= (2/18)/(-1/11) \\ &= 2/18 \times -11/1 \\ &= -11/9 \\ &= -1.22 \end{aligned}$$

    c. | Price | Quantity | Total Revenue |
        |-------|----------|---------------|
        | 4 | 12 | 48 |
        | 5 | 10 | 50 |
        | 6 | 8 | 48 |
        | 7 | 6 | 42 |

    At a price of $5, revenue reaches its peak. This is also where point price elasticity is 1, as shown in part a. of this problem.

3. a. When price changes by 1, quantity will change by 10 in the opposite direction. When income changes by 1, quantity will change by .5 in the same direction.

    b. Point elasticity:
    $$\begin{aligned} Q &= 100 - (10)(7) + (.5)(50) \\ &= 100 - 70 + 25 \\ &= 55 \end{aligned}$$

    Slope $= -10$

    $\varepsilon_p = (-10) \times (7/55) = -1.27$

    Arc elasticity, between $P = 7$ and $P = 6$:
    at $P = 6$, $Q = 100 - (10)(6) + (.5)(50) = 65$

    $E_p = (65 - 55)/(65 + 55) \div (6 - 7)/(6 + 7) = -1.08$

c. Point elasticity
Slope = 0.5

$\varepsilon_y = (.5) \times (50/55) = 0.45$

Arc elasticity, between Y = 50 and Y = 60
at Y = 60, Q = 100 - (10)(7) + (.5)(60) = 60

$$E_y = (60 - 55)/(60 + 55) \div (60 - 50)/(60 + 50) = 0.48$$

d. Point elasticity
Q = 100 - (10)(8) + (.5)(70) = 55

$\varepsilon_p = (-10) \times (8/55) = -1.45$

Arc elasticity, between P = 8 and P = 7

Q = 100 - (10)(7) + (.5)(70) = 65

$E_p = (65 - 55)/(65 + 55) \div (7 - 8)/(7 + 8) = -1.25$

4. a. At P = 7, Q = 30 - (2)(7) = 16

Slope = -2

$\varepsilon_p = (-2) \times (7/16) = -0.88$

b. At P = 5, Q = 30 - (2)(5) = 20
       P = 6, Q = 30 - (2)(6) = 18

$E_p = (18 - 20)/(18 + 20) \div (6 - 5)/(6 + 5) = -0.58$

c. Elasticity will be the same. Equation is now
Q = 3000 - 200P

At P = 7, Q = 3000 - (200)(7) = 1600

Slope = -200

$\varepsilon_p = -200 \times (7/1600) = -0.88$

5. a. $$-2.5 = \frac{(x - 4000)}{(x + 4000)} \div \frac{(63 - 70)}{(63 + 70)}$$

x = 5212

At P = 70, TR = 4000 x 70 = 280,000
      P = 63, TR = 5212 x 63 = 328,356

Revenue will increase, because demand curve is elastic.

6.   a. $-3 = \dfrac{(x - 3000)}{(x + 3000)} \div \dfrac{(22 - 25)}{(22 + 25)}$

     $x = 4421$

   b. $.3 = \dfrac{(x - 3000)}{(x + 3000)} \div \dfrac{(24 - 28)}{(24 + 28)}$

     $x = 2865$

7.   If price elasticity is -4, and the Redbirds wish to increase attendance from 50,000 to 80,000, the price (x) must be:

$$-4 = \dfrac{(80000 - 50000)}{(80000 + 50000)} \div \dfrac{(x - 30)}{(x + 30)}$$

   $x = 26.73$

If price is lowered from \$30 to 27, and attendance rises from 50,000 to 60,000, price elasticity is:

$$E_p = \dfrac{(60000 - 50000)}{(60000 + 50000)} \div \dfrac{(27 - 30)}{(27 + 30)}$$

   $= -1.727$

8.   Arc price elasticity for spreadsheet program:

$$E_p = \dfrac{(120 - 100)}{(120 + 100)} , \dfrac{(350 - 400)}{(350 + 400)}$$

   $= -1.36$

Arc cross elasticity for graphics program:

$$E_x = \dfrac{(56 - 50)}{(56 + 50)} , \dfrac{(350 - 400)}{(350 + 400)}$$

   $= -0.85$

The quantity demanded for spreadsheets increased due to the price change. The price elasticity is greater than (absolute) 1, and therefore revenue will rise from \$40,000 to \$42,000.

The graphics program is a complementary commodity to the spreadsheet program, and its quantity sold benefited from the price decrease in the spreadsheet program. The cross-elasticity is -0.85 (the negative sign shows complementarity), and is quite strong.

9.   Demand Elasticity

Price	Quantity	Arc	Point	Total Revenue	Marginal Revenue
7.00	100			700	
6.50	200	-9.00	-6.50	1300	6.00
6.00	300	-5.00	-4.00	1800	5.00
5.50	400	-3.29	-2.75	2200	4.00
5.00	500	-2.33	-2.00	2500	3.00
4.50	600	-1.73	-1.50	2700	2.00
4.00	700	-1.31	-1.14	2800	1.00
3.50	800	-1.00	-0.88	2800	0.00
3.00	900	-0.76	-0.67	2700	-1.00
2.50	1000	-0.58	-0.50	2500	-2.00
2.00	1100	-0.43	-0.36	2200	-3.00
1.50	1200	-0.30	-0.25	1800	-4.00

10.   a.   Negative: television sets and VCRs are complements.
      b.   Positive: rye bread and whole-wheat bread are substitutes.
      c.   Negative: construction of residential housing and furniture purchases are complements.
      d.   Probably zero: breakfast cereal and men's shirts are unrelated products. However, they may be thought of a substitutes in the competition for a consumer's budget dollars.

11.   a.   The price elasticity for shoes in the U.S. is 0.7. However, the elasticity for Brown Shoe Company's shoes may be higher, since a particular make of shoes has more substitutes than shoes in general. The exact demand elasticity for Brown's product is not known, but it could easily be greater than 1 (or less than negative one), and thus a price decrease could lead to an increase in revenue.
      b.   The quantity of shoes sold in the U.S. would rise by 9%.

12.   1.5 = -30%/-20%   UBS would lose 30% of its sales.

13.   a.   There is a 14.3% decrease in price. With a 20% increase in quantity, this implies an elasticity coefficient of -1.4.
      b.   Syrup is a complementary good in relation to ice cream. Cross elasticity would measure this effect.
              +0.1/-0.143 = -0.7
      c.   The coefficient of cross elasticity is -0.7, confirming complementarity of syrup to ice cream. The coefficient is quite high, and thus one could conclude that the two products are fairly close complements.
      d.   Yes, revenues for both ice cream and syrup rise. Unless costs rise more quickly (a very dubious conclusion), this action should increase the supermarket's profit.

14. In computing the elasticities, remember that an elasticity measure can be calculated only if all other things remain constant.

Price elasticities

Months 3-4	-1.00	$\dfrac{20/(220+240)/2}{-10/(120+110)/2}$
Months 4-5	-0.96	$\dfrac{-10/(240+230)/2}{5/(110+115)/2}$
Months 7-8	-0.49	$\dfrac{10/(220+230)/2}{-10/(115+105)/2}$

Cross elasticities

Months 1-2	0.45	$\dfrac{10/(200+210)/2}{15/(130+145)/2}$
Months 5-6	0.46	$\dfrac{-15/(230+215)/2}{-20/(145+125)/2}$
Month 9-10	0.79	$\dfrac{-15/(235+220)/2}{-10/(125+115)/2}$

Income elasticities

Months 2-3	0.95	$\dfrac{10/(210+220)/2}{200/(4000+4200)/2}$
Months 6-7	0.49	$\dfrac{5/(215+220)/2}{200/(4200+4400)/2}$
Months 8-9	0.48	$\dfrac{5/(230+235)/2}{200/(4400+4600)/2}$

15. a.   1800   2000 - 200

   b. $0   2000 = 2000 - 20P
        $100   0 = 2000 - 20P
        $25   1500 = 2000 - 20P

   c.   Q = 2000 - 20P
        20P = 2000 - Q
          P = 100 - .05Q
         TR = PQ = 100Q - .05Q^2

         MR = 100 - .1Q

   d.   Q = 2000 - 20(70) = 600
        TR = 600 x 70 = 42000
                or

$$TR = 100Q - .05Q^2$$
$$= 60000 - .05(600)^2$$
$$= 60000 - 18000$$
$$= 42000$$

$$MR = 100 - .1(600)$$
$$= 100 - 60 = 40$$

e. $\varepsilon = dQ/dP \times P/Q$
$$= 20 \times 70/600$$
$$= 1400/600 = 2.33$$

f. $Q = 2000 - 20(60)$
$$= 800$$

$$TR = 800 \times 60 = 48000$$

$$MR = 100 - .1(800)$$
$$= 20$$

$$\varepsilon = 20 \times 60/800$$
$$= 1200/800 = 1.5$$

g. At $\varepsilon = 1$ $MR = 0$

$$0 = 100 - .1Q$$
$$.1Q = 100$$
$$Q = 1000$$

Proof: $1000 = 2000 - 20P$
$$20P = 1000$$
$$P = 50$$

$$\varepsilon = 20 \times 50/1000 = 1000/1000 = 1$$

CHAPTER 5
DEMAND ESTIMATION

QUESTIONS

1. Time series data: Information concerning a particular variable over time at specified intervals (e.g., weekly, monthly, quarterly, annually). For example, the average monthly price of corn, the total quantity demanded of pizza per week, annual income per capita.

   Cross-sectional data: Information concerning a particular variable at a specific point in time for a given unit of observation. For example, the average price of corn in April 1995 for all countries in the world who produce this good, the total quantity of pizza demanded on November 21, 1995, by each college campus in the United States, income per capita in 1995 for all countries that belong to the United Nations.

2. In both cases, as many of the price and non-price factors that influence demand should be included. However, in the demand equation for consumer durables, some variable indicating the cost or availability of credit should be used. This particular variable would not be considered an important factor in the demand for fast-moving consumer goods.

   (Instructors may wish to discuss other possible differences such as the inclusion of a dummy variable indicating a period of recession in the time-series analysis of consumer durables.)

3. A deterministic model can be represented by an algebraic equation containing the usual dependent variable (Y) and one or more independent variables (X_i). A probabilistic model can also be represented in this fashion, but it also must include some random factor (U_i) that takes into account the probability that the value of Y will vary (randomly) relative to the value that it is expected to assume given the values of X and the equation's coefficients.

4. R^2 is a measure of the explanatory power of the regression model. It is also referred to as a measure of "the goodness of fit" (of the regression line through the scatter of data points). Specifically, it indicates the percentage of the variation in the dependent variable Y explained or accounted for by the variation in the independent variable(s) X.

   Other factors held constant, time series data generally produce a higher R^2 than cross-sectional data because both dependent and independent variables often move together over time simply because of some upward trend. A good example of this is a time-series analysis of aggregate consumption regressed on aggregate disposable income. Regression analysis of this consumption function commonly produce R^2 of .95 and above.

5. Cross-sectional data tend to produce a lower R^2 the greater the disaggregation of the data. For example, a regression model of the demand for a product using data on individuals or households will generally result in a lower R^2 than the same one using data on counties, cities, or states. The more disaggregated the data, the more difficult it is to account for the variation in quantity demanded because of the pronounced impact of the idiosyncrasies of individual behavior. These idiosyncracies among individuals tend to offset each other when consumer behavior is aggregated.

   One has to be careful about using a higher R^2 as the key indicator of a superior regression model. This is particularly the case when the model with the higher R^2 has more independent variables. As explained in the chapter, R^2 will increase automatically when more independent variables are added. In order to assess the relative superiority of two or more regression equations, one has to look at other tests such as the t-test and also to use one's experience and common sense in judging each variable's impact on the dependent variable.

6. a. State the null hypothesis and the alternative hypothesis.
    b. Select the level of significance (e.g., a = .05) and the associated critical value of t (using the t table).
    c. Compute the t value (if the software package does not do it for you).
    d. Compare the t value with the critical value. If the former exceeds the latter, reject the null hypothesis. If it does not, then do not reject the null hypothesis.

    The "rule of 2" is useful, because in most cases, the critical value of t is approximately 2 for the .05 level of significance, the level most commonly used in economic research.

7. The F-test is a measure of the statistical significance of the entire regression equation. If it is used in simple regression (i.e., for a regression equation with only one independent variable), then in effect it provides the same test as the t-test for this particular variable. The F-test is much more useful, when two or more independent variables are used. It can then test whether all of these variables taken together are statistically significant from zero, leaving the t-test to determine whether each variable taken separately is statistically significant.

8. Multicollinearity occurs when two or more independent variables in a regression equation are highly correlated with each other. An indication of this problem occurs when a regression equation passes the F-test but fails to produce individual variables that pass the t-test. Also, when the correlation coefficients among the independent variables are high (i.e., about .7 or more), researchers often consider this to be a problem in the equation. As explained in the chapter, if this problem is serious, it will cause an upward bias in the t values of the independent variables. This in turn will make it more difficult to reject the null hypothesis.

9. The identification problem refers to the difficulty of clearly identifying the demand equation because of the effects of both supply and demand that are often reflected in data used in the analysis. As explained in the chapter, if this problem exists, it could lead to a bias in the sensitivity of quantity demanded relative to price.

PROBLEMS

1. a. Whenever new products are introduced, it is clearly difficult to use regression analysis to estimate their demand because they have no history. If an analysis insists on using time-series data, then data on a similar product (e.g., VCRs, TVs, video cameras) might be used as a proxy for the demand for this product. Cross-sectional data may be generated from consumer surveys, but analysis should take into account the difficulty consumers might have in discussing an unfamiliar product. Nonetheless, they could be asked such questions as their tastes or preferences about such a product, their willingness to buy it at different prices etc. Focus groups or telephone surveys are two common ways that companies obtain such information.

    b. The usual variables such as price, amount spent on advertising, quantity demanded, level of aggregate economic activity should be gathered for this study. Key variables might well be the price of competing products (e.g., video rental, pay-per-view) and complementary products (price of the CDs).

    c. The emergence of the multimedia PC illustrates how the introduction of new technology can quickly affect the market for a product. Why would anyone want to buy a product that can only read a CD when it is now possible to buy a PC that can do the same thing? Of course, there is the initial price difference. The initial price of $1,000 for the new CD player is about half the price of a basic multimedia PC. Nonetheless, the new CD product was announced in 1992, but never really caught on in the marketplace. We suspect that one of the reasons is the multimedia PC.

2. Price: Average price of the furniture. If the demand for different models or types (e.g., dining room, bedroom, living room furniture) is estimated, then the average price of each type must be used.

    Tastes and Preferences: Amount of advertising expenditures. (Information about buyers' background such as age, occupation, level of education, could be used as proxy variables for taste and preferences for different models or styles of furniture.)

    Price of Related Products: If this is the demand for the furniture of a particular company, then its competitors' prices could be included. Otherwise, a key "complementary" product would be housing prices... or perhaps, housing sales, new home sales etc.)

    Income: Per capita income, disposable income, personal income, GNP.

    Cost or Availability of Credit: The key question is which interest rate to use. Interest rates on major credit cards might be useful, but they do not vary too often. Perhaps, the prime rate or the rate on a selected short-term government security such as the one-year T-bill rate could be used. Mortgage rates could be used but they would tend to affect demand for furniture via their impact on housing sales.

    Number of buyers: Number of households (as opposed to individuals) would probably be the best measure of this variable.

    Future Expectations: This is the most difficult variable to measure. Instructors may simply ask their students to "brainstorm" for possible measures.

    Other Possible Factors: Instructors: we leave this for you to open for possible class discussion.

3.

Variable	Coefficient	Std. Error	T-Stat.	2-Tail Sig.
C	91.322086	11.404689	8.0074157	0.000
Price	-0.0060524	0.0009809	-6.1701311	0.000

R-squared	0.760338	Mean of dependent var	21.07143
Adjusted R-squared	0.740366	S.D. of dependent var	4.843144
S.E. of regression	2.467789	Sum of squared resid	73.07979
Durbin-Watson stat	1.758028	F-statistic	38.07052
Log likelihood	-31.43260		

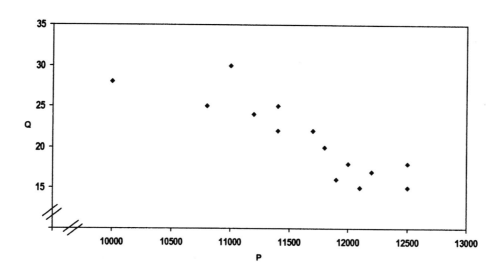

Month	Price	Quantity
January	$12,500	15
February	$12,200	17
March	$11,900	16
April	$12,000	18
May	$11,800	20
June	$12,500	18
July	$11,700	22
August	$12,100	15
September	$11,400	22
October	$11,400	25
November	$11,200	24
December	$11,000	30
January	$10,800	25
February	$10,000	28

Regression Output

Constant	91.32209
Std. Err. of Y Est.	2.467789
R. Squared	0.760338
No. of Observations	14
Degrees of Freedom	12

X Coefficient(s)	-0.00605
Std. Err. of Y Est.	0.000981

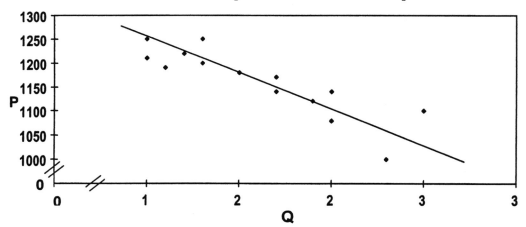

Scatter Graph—Automobile Dealership

4. $Q = -5200 - 42P + 20P_x + 5.2I + .20A + .25M$

   $= -5200 - 42(500) + 20(600) + 5.2(5500) + .20(10,000) + .25(5000)$

   $= -5200 - 2100 + 1200 + 28,600 + 2000 + 1250$

$Q = 17,650$

   a. $E_P = -\dfrac{21,000}{17,650} = -1.18$

   $E_X = \dfrac{12,000}{17,650} = .68$

   $E_I = \dfrac{28,600}{17,650} = 1.62$

   $E_A = \dfrac{2,000}{17,650} = .113$

   $E_M = \dfrac{1,250}{17,650} = .07$

   b.   This firm should be very concerned because income elasticity is relatively high (i.e., the product is "superior").

   c.   This firm might want to cut its price to increase its sales because the product is price elastic (although only barely). However, if its leading competitor retaliates, the firm must expect to be affect substantially because its cross price elasticity is relatively high.

   d.   The R^2 indicates that about 55 percent of the variation in quantity demanded can be explained by the variation in the independent variables. The F of 4.88 indicates that this result is statistically significant at the .05 level.

5. $Q = +15,000 - 2.80P + 150A + .3P_{PC} + .35P_M + .2P_C$

$= +15,000 - 2.80(7,000) + 150(52) + .3(4,000) + .35(15,000) + .2(8,000)$

$= +15,000 - 19,600 + 7,800 + 1200 + 5,250 + 1,600$

$Q = 11,250$

a. $E_P = \dfrac{19,600}{11,250} = -1.74$

$E_A = \dfrac{7,800}{11,250} = .69$

$E_{PC} = \dfrac{1,200}{11,250} = .10$

$E_M = \dfrac{1,600}{11,250} = .47$

$E_C = \dfrac{1,200}{11,250} = .14$

According to the regression results, the key variable is price. The price of a minicomputer does seem to have some impact on the workstation's sales (i.e., cross elasticity = .47) but the results indicate that the price of the PC as well as the competitor's price does not appear to have much of an impact.

The results indicate that customers are extremely price sensitive. Therefore, the firm should be very careful about how it prices the product. If it also happens to be selling PCs and minicomputers, then the prices of these products do not seem to have much of an impact on the sales of its workstations. However, it is quite possible that a price reduction in workstations could have an substantial impact on the sales of PCs and minicomputers. However, the above regression results cannot tell us what this impact might be.

A one-tail test can be used for each of the variables. The use of a two-tail test would not change any of the findings. The t test indicates that the impact of the competitor's price on the product in question is not statistically significant.

Interest rates might well have an impact on sales. However, it would be more appropriate in a time-series analysis of sales. The price relative to performance (e.g., price per MIP) might also be an important variable. However, it too would be more appropriate in a time series analysis. And unlike the case of interest rates, the time series data on this variable might not be available simply because the workstation is a relatively new product.

6. $Q = 40 - 1.1(55) + 1.5(20) + .32(31) + .5(10) + .1(50)$

$Q = 29.42 = 29,420$

a.   Probably not because the income elasticity is fairly low.

$$E_I = \frac{9.92}{29.42} = .34$$

b. The regression results indicate that the firm should not be worried because the cross price elasticity is only .17.

c. Advertising is fairly effective because advertising elasticity is 1.02.

d. This firm should consider lowering its price to gain market share because its price elasticity is relatively high.

$$E_P = \frac{-60.5}{29.42} = -2.05$$

Moreover, because the cross price elasticity is so low, any retaliation by its competitor would not have much of an impact on its sales. (However, note that the coefficient of the competitor's price is not statistically significant.)

e. At the 95% confidence level, the forecasted interval is 29.42 + or - 1.976(2.8). That is, it is between 23.89 and 34.95.

7. a. The coefficient of P_j (1.2) is greater than that of P_a (.75). This implies that consumers perceive Japanese luxury cars (e.g., the Acura, Lexus, Infiniti, and Diamante) as being closer substitutes for European luxury cars (e.g., BMW, Volvo, Mercedes, and Audi) than are American luxury cars (e.g., Lincoln Continental and Cadillac). Taste and perception as to what is a substitute for a particular product is very subjective. However, we do recall that the auto magazines were very skeptical about whether the Japanese could ever supplant the perception in American consumers' minds about the status, quality, and image of the German luxury cars. Recent statistics indicate how successful the Japanese have been in taking market share away from the likes of BMW and Mercedes in the U.S. luxury car market. However, the instructor may wish to comment on the tremendous success of certain 1992 Cadillac models in recapturing the interest of American consumers (particularly those in their 40s—as opposed to the typical Cadillac buyer in his or her 50s and 60s).

b. The coefficient of I (1.6) is greater than one, indicating as expected that this is a luxury or superior product.

c. The absolute value of the price coefficient (.93) indicates that demand is relatively inelastic. This is not surprising, given the income levels of those who tend to buy these types of cars.

CHAPTER 6
FORECASTING

QUESTIONS

1. Corporate management sets objectives for the company's profit, revenue and other measures, based on economic forecasts, available and obtainable resources and changes in productivity. Objectives are the results the company wishes to attain in the future. Both long-term and short-term objectives can be stated.

    Forecasts are calculations of future values of certain variables (sales, revenue, profit) based on past results and assumptions about future conditions.

    A plan utilizes forecasts and designs corporate actions and policies to attain the objectives set by management.

2. It is well known that forecasts, economic and other, are not always accurate. But to have knowledgeable people (even with incomplete knowledge) make estimates about the future will decrease the uncertainty with which decision makers must deal. Knowing something about the future aids management in the decision making process.

3. Not necessarily. While more accuracy is better than less, a cost is usually involved in making forecasts more accurate. If the additional cost is greater that the benefit obtained from additional accuracy, then the additional work to improve a forecast should not be undertaken and the additional costs should not be incurred.

4. Qualitative: usually not based on quantitative historical data although results may be in numerical form.
    | Methods: | expert opinion |
    | | opinion polls and market research |
    | | surveys of spending plans |
    | Quantitative: | usually based on numerical historical data, and forecast numerical results. |
    | Methods: | projections |
    | | econometric models |

5. a. Jury of executive opinion. Opinions come from experts in the forecast area, but in a panel discussion the most persuasive person may not be the most knowledgeable one. This methods is often used to forecast sales, costs, production, profits, etc.

    b. Delphi method. Forecasts are made by experts. The experts' opinions are usually obtained over the telephone or by writing. Since the experts generally do not meet, there will not be any undue influence exercised by the more articulate members of the panel. However, since this method is frequently used in far-out technological forecasting, it may actually not be possible to forecast events not yet conceived. Further, because of the nature of the forecasts, they are often rather unreliable. This forecasting method is usually employed for forecasting of technological changes and demand, and market conditions far into the future.

    c. Opinion polls. These are surveys conducted with population samples that are not experts but whose activities may determine future events. Since only samples are surveyed, it is essential that the sample be representative and the questions are carefully stated. Opinion polls are usually expensive. Another problem is that respondents' answers may reflect what they think their opinions should be rather than what they are.

6.   There is a definite decline in the leading indicators' index forecasting a decline in economic activity. Since the timing of the lead varies substantially, all that can be said is that a recession should have started in the latter part of 1990. In fact, it actually did.

7.   a.   Manufacturers' new orders, non defense capital goods, will translate into actual production and expenditures some time later. Thus they forecast economic activity.

    b.   The index of industrial production reflects the actual economic activity at the time it is reported.

    c.   The prime rate reflects changes in the demand and supply of loanable funds. Only when such changes are experienced by banks, will they change the rate. They may wait until they are certain that the change is not a temporary event, but will have some permanency.

8.   A major problem is that, while leading indicators are a fairly good forecaster of changes in economic activity, they are not reliable at forecasting the timing of troughs or peaks. The lead time can be as little as two months or as much as ten months or more. Usually, three consecutive months of declines or increases are accepted as indicators of change in economic direction. However, three months may be a long time to wait before the signal is accepted. Also, some of the series are revised a month or two after they are first published. These revisions can, and often have, been large enough to change the direction of the indicator index.

9.   Naive forecasting methods are those which project trends without investigating the causes of the changes. Projections using compound growth factors, the extrapolation of trends from graphic observations and time-series analysis are all considered to be naive forecasting methods.

10.   From the beginning of 1626 to the end of 1999 is 374 years, or 748 semiannual periods. At 3% semiannually, $24 would grow to $96,040,700,972.

11.   The compound growth rate method will give reasonable results if the growth rate of the past is expected to continue into the future. However, the compound growth rate calculation is usually based on only the first and last historical data points. If either one of these represents an abnormal result, or if the year-to-year growth rate changes exhibit a decreasing or increasing trend, then the CGR forecast could be very misleading.

12.   If the vertical scale of a graph is in terms of logarithms, while the horizontal scale is arithmetic, a graph showing observations over time will tell us something about the growth rate. On a logarithmic scale, changes of the same percentage magnitude will plot on a straight line. Thus, a straight upward line on a "semi-log" scale will indicate that year-to-year percentage growth is constant. If the line is increasing at a decreasing rate, then growth is diminishing; if the line is rising at an increasing rate, then growth is increasing.

13.   Moving average projections: A moving average of past data is used to forecast the next period. The number of past observations to include in the moving average must be specified. Thus, if a 1996 quantity is to be forecast with a three-year moving average, then 1993-1995 data are used. The larger the number of past data in the moving average the greater will be the smoothing effect.

Exponential smoothing: The moving-average method gives the same weight to each of the past observations employed in the moving average. On the other hand, the exponential smoothing method makes it possible to weight the most recent observation more heavily, and allow for decreasing weights to be given to observations further in the distant past.

Both of these techniques can be used for very short-term forecasting in cases where there is no pronounced upward or downward trend, and where fluctuations from period to period are random.

14. Naive forecasting models forecast the future trends without explaining the reason for these changes. Econometric forecasting models, on the other hand, include causative independent variables in their analysis in order to explain the reasons for changes in future direction.

Econometric models tend to be much a more complex forecasting device than naive models. Where past changes are good predictors of the future, naive models may be able to do an adequate forecasting job with a great deal less effort and cost.

15. b. and d. The purpose of leading economic indicators is the determination of turning points in economic activity. Survey methods (such as the survey of consumer sentiment or capital expenditures) are also used to determine changes in economic activity in the short run.

Trend projections do not predict ups and downs in economic activity but forecast the continuation of past trends. Lagging economic indicators confirm what is happening in the economy but would be too late to predict a turn in economic activity.

PROBLEMS

1. Compound growth rate is 16%. This answer can be obtained with an electronic calculator or as follows:

    1050150/50000 = 2.1003. From table 1.a. in text appendix, rate is 16%.

    At a 10% growth rate, sales will be 1,691,277 five years from now. This can be obtained with an electronic calculator, or from table 1.a. The five-year 10% factor in the table is 1.6105. When multiplied by 1,050,150, the result is 1,691,277.

2. a. $1000 + 100(5) = 1500$

    b.   Without a seasonal factor, quarterly sales in 2000 would be 375.

    With seasonal factors:

1st quarter	375 x 0.8	300
2d quarter	375 x 1.0	375
3d quarter	375 x 1.25	468.75
4th quarter	375 x 0.95	356.25
		1,500

3. a.   16% (more exact answer is 15.98%)

    b.   If growth calculated at 16%:   2000   1,012,680
         2001   1,174,709

    c.   14% (more exact answer is 14.02)

    d.   If growth calculated at 14%:   2000   995,220
         2001   1,134,551

    e.   The annual growth rate in sales from 1986 to 1995 is decreasing:

1991	20.0%
1992	18.8
1993	18.3
1994	16.8
1995	16.1
1996	15.0
1997	14.0
1998	12.9
1999	12.1

    On average the decrease in the rate of growth was 1% point per year. If this trend were to continue, the forecasts for 1996 and 1997 would be:

2000	11%	969,030
2001	10%	1,065,933

4. a. 7.7%

    b. 906,000 x 1.077 = 975,762

    c. Annual growth rates appear to decrease at first, then increase:

1989	10.0%	1995	6.0%
1990	9.1	1996	7.0
1991	7.9	1997	8.0
1992	6.9	1998	9.0
1993	6.0	1999	10.0
1994	5.1		

    If the recent upward trend is expected to continue, then an 11% increase to $1,005,660 could be a good forecast. A more conservative forecast would be to take, for instance, the average of 1997-1999, which is 9%, and project 2000 sales to be $987,540.

5. a. A least-square time-series trend line is:
        176.667 + 20.5879t

    The past 10 years describe a straight line. Thus, if it is expected that 2000 would continue on a similar trend, then

    176.667 + 20.5879(11) = 403, could be projected with sufficient confidence.

    b. Using exponential smoothing for the entire series, with a factor of 0.7, would give the following result:

1991	200 x .7 + 200 x .3 = 200
1992	215 x .7 + 200 x .3 = 211
1993	237 x .7 + 211 x .3 = 229
1994	260 x .7 + 229 x .3 = 251
1995	278 x .7 + 251 x .3 = 270
1996	302 x .7 + 270 x .3 = 292
1997	320 x .7 + 292 x .3 = 312
1998	345 x .7 + 312 x .3 = 335
1999	360 x .7 + 335 x .3 = 353
2000	382 x .7 + 353 x .3 = 373

    If we had started the smoothing procedure just one period back (utilizing the actual number rather than a previous forecast), the result may have been somewhat different. Suppose we had started with 1998, and for 1999 predicted using actual 1998 and actual 1997 numbers to predict 1999:

1999	360 x .7 + 345 x .3 = 356
2000	382 x .7 + 356 x .3 = 374

    It can be seen that the difference in the two forecasts is quite small. Forecasting with exponential smoothing is not a good method in this case. There is a pronounced upward trend in the series, which makes the exponential smoothing method inferior. Scanning the numbers, it is obvious that each year's forecast has been too low.

6.   a.   Three-month centered moving average:

February	$513
March	517
April	520
May	540
June	573
July	603
August	603
September	583
October	547
November	513

b.

October	$550
November	510
December	480
January forecast	$513

c.   In general, since the annual pattern is quite seasonal, the moving average forecast is not a good one. It is difficult to say whether the January forecast is reliable. If there is an overall upward trend, then the $513 for next January may not be a bad forecast. However, forecasting February from the data is more risky. The three-month moving average (using November and December actuals and the January forecast) forecast would be $501. This is opposite of the previous year's pattern in which February had higher sales than January.

7.   a. $Q = 10000 + 60(160) - 100(40) + 50(35)$
             $= 10000 + 9600 - 4000 + 1750$
             $= 17350$

b. $Q = 10000 + 9600 - 4000 + 50(32)$
             $= 17200$

$Q = 10000 + 9600 - 4000 + 50(36)$
      $= 17400$

c. $Q = 10000 + 9600 - 100(37) + 50(32)$
             $= 17500$

d. $60(160) = 9600$
       $60(140) = 8400$

With an index of 140 rather than 160, quantity would decrease by 1200 units.

8.   a.   Linear trend:
             Current GDP $3540.5 + 306.1538 \times t$
             Real GDP $5083.227 + 137.8497 \times t$

b.   Exponential trend:
             Current GDP $3761.609 \times (1.05803)^t$
             Real GDP $5123.597 \times (1.023524)^t$

c.

Current GDP ($bill)		Linear Trend		Exponential Trend	
	Actual	Estimate	Variance	Estimate	Variance
1996	7,662	7,520	142	7,832	-170
1997	8,111	7,827	284	8,286	-175

Real GDP ($bill)		Linear Trend		Exponential Trend	
	Actual	Estimate	Variance	Estimate	Variance
1996	6,995	6,875	120	6,932	63
1997	7,270	7,013	257	7,095	175

d.   None of these lines appears to be a very good predictor. Gross Domestic Product is a result of many influences in the economy, and thus cannot be reliably forecasted by a simple trend projection.

9.

January	55.4	July	87.5
February	65.2	August	78.4
March	79.9	September	93.9
April	104.3	October	109.6
May	105.2	November	140.6
June	96.4	December	151.8

10.   a.   (1) $220036.2 + 2352.219 \times t$
     (2) $220825.9249 \times (1.009705)^t$
     (3) .983296%

b.

		Linear Trend		Exponential Trend		Growth Rate	
	Actual	Estimate	Variance	Estimate	Variance	Estimate	Variance
1997	267901	267081	820	267880	21	268063	-162
1998	270290	269433	857	270480	-190	270699	-409

d.   The exponential trend appears to give the best forecast. An exponential trend is actually a percentage increase.

11.   a.   (1) $703.0381 + 743.7536 \times t$
     (2) $2241.0639 \times (1.1274)^t$
     (3) $-6820.91 + 2.359605 \times GDP$

b.

Actual	15,307
Straight-line estimate	12,603
Variance	2,704
Exponential estimate	15,265
Variance	42
Regression estimate	13,257
Variance	2,050

The exponential trend gives the best 1998 estimate.

CHAPTER 7 AND APPENDIXES
THE THEORY AND ESTIMATION OF PRODUCTION

QUESTIONS

1. The short run production function contains at least one fixed input. In the long run production function, there are no fixed inputs, all inputs are variable. In a manufacturing company, a short run production function involves the increase in labor inputs (e.g., working three shifts instead of two). If the firm expands its factory, or builds a new one, it would be considered an example of its long run production function.

2. The law of diminishing returns: As additional units of variable input are added to a fixed input, at some point the additional output (marginal product) resulting from this addition starts to diminish.

   Another way to consider this law is to recognize that when it takes effect, a firm has to add increasingly more of the variable input in order to increase the additional output by a constant amount.

   This law is considered a short-run phenomenon in economic theory because it requires at least one of the inputs used by the firm to be held constant.

3. Stage I ends and Stage II begins at the point of maximum AP. Stage II ends and Stage III begins at the point of maximum output (i.e., when MP = 0). The law of diminishing returns occurs just before Stage I ends. As the MP starts to diminish it intersects AP at AP's highest value.

4. Adhering to the MRP=MLC (or MRP=MFC) rule is an example of equalizing at the margin. As long as the benefit of using an additional unit of input (i.e., MRP) is greater than its cost (i.e., MLC), it pays for the firm to employ an extra unit.

   Once MLC exceeds MRP, it no longer pays for the firm to do so. At the margin, the firm will stop adding inputs at the point where the additional benefit (MRP) is just equal to the additional cost (MLC).

5. Returns to scale is a measure of the increase in a firm's output relative to an increase in all of its inputs. It is considered a long-run phenomenon in economic theory because all inputs are allowed to change.

6. Perhaps the firm is not following the rule at first. However, after completing the program, the trainee is expected to increase his or her productivity sufficiently to exceed the costs associated with the hiring and training.

7. If marginal product is greater than average product, average product increases. If it is less than average product, average product decreases. If it is equal to average product, then average product is either at a maximum or a minimum. In the short-run production function, since marginal product starts off as greater than average product and then falls below average product, we can assume that at the "cross-over point," when MP = AP, AP is at its maximum.

8. A firm may find itself in Stage I or III of its short run production function simply because of the dictates of demand. In other words, the range of its output in Stage II may simply not match the amount that people are willing to buy.

   Instructors may wish to discuss the possible reasons why this could happen (e.g., incorrect demand forecasts, inappropriate capital expenditures etc.).

9. It is sometimes difficult to measure productivity, particularly for individuals. Economists use fairly broad measures of productivity such as the market value of output divided by the number of workers. However, not everyone in an organization can be directly associated with this value.

   When the output is a service rather than a good, it sometimes is difficult to quantify this service. Furthermore, the quality of a service is often as important (if not more important) than the quantity. And in many cases, labor time spent with a customer is directly related to this quality of service. If this is the case, then the quantity and quality of a person's efforts may be in conflict with each other. The examples below are intended to get students to think about these issues.

   a. Education: An obvious quantitative measure of teacher productivity would be number of students in a class. But is there a point at which the increase in class size interferes with learning? Moreover, what about such qualitative measures as the performance of the students in the subject being taught?

   b. Government: Number of forms processed, number of inquiries answered, number of audits conducted are all examples of output. However, here again, the conflict between quantity and quality may need to be considered.

   c. Manufacturing: Manufacturing industries conform very closely to the traditional economic view of the production function. "Q" could be the soap, toothpaste, computers, or....widgets.

   d. Finance and Insurance: It is little easier to measure output here than in the case of education and government. The only caution is that output in terms of customers served may not be as important as the amount of revenue generated per customer. Consider the case of a teller who spends 10 minutes explaining to a customer why it takes 6 days for an out-of-town check to clear versus one who spends the same amount of time helping a customer buy a $50,000 certificate of deposit.

10. A question that we found opens the class up to some interesting discussion. We leave the answer for each instructor and class to decide.

11. The two regression methods used in estimating production functions are the cross-section and time-series techniques. To do a cross-section analysis, data are collected for different plants at the same point in time. In a time-series analysis the data are for one plant or firm over a period of time.

   In a time-series analysis, the analyst must assure himself/herself that there have been no technological changes in the plant during the time-frame of the study. If any of the data used in this analysis are in monetary terms, then an adjustment for changes in prices must be made. Also, there is an implicit assumption that the plant is operating with an optimal combination of resources. However, an advantage is that the observations are for the same plant, and that the data have probably been collected in a consistent and comparable manner.

The cross-section regression analysis overcomes the problem of technology changing over time, but it creates a problem in implicitly assuming that all plants in the sample are operating at a similar technological level. If monetary quantities are used anywhere in the analysis, then an adjustment for different price or wage levels across different geographical areas must be made. Again, there is an assumption that all plants operate at an optimum combination of resources.

Usually (as in cost studies), the time-series analysis is employed for short-run production functions and assumes that the size of the plant (as well as technology) has not changed. The cross-section method is used in analyzing long-run production functions since it permits for comparison of plants of different capacities.

12.   Since we will be studying a single steel mill, we will employ a time-series regression analysis. We will collect monthly data over a period of three years when there was little or no change in the technology or size of the plant. If the mill produces only one product, then the dependent variable Q (quantity) will be the monthly tonnage produced. If there is more than one product, a weighting device will have to be employed to obtain the production quantity. The most important, and possibly only essential, independent variable would be direct manpower. Since there is probably some fluctuation in the hours worked from month to month, a monthly labor hour figure will be better than an employment figure.

Different forms of a production function should be attempted. Probably a quadratic or a cubic equation should be fitted. Also an exponential function should be attempted.

Other independent variables which may be significant could be indirect labor-hours, and tons of iron ore processed during a month.

The call center and the steel mill would ostensibly involve the same general categories of inputs: labor and capital. For example, in the case of the call center, the capital would be the office facilities, the telephone premise equipment and computers and all of the other computers and switches that go along with a modern call center operation. The capital involved in a steel mill would be all of its plant and equipment and property. The key difference between the production functions of these two operations involves the measurement of output rather than inputs. How does one actually measure the "output" of a call center operation ... the number of calls, the length of time of each call? Perhaps, but the problem is that the quality of the product may differ depending on the length of the call. Nonetheless, this does not stop efficiency experts in call center operations from using such measures of output. This problem does not exist in the production of goods such as steel.

Key learning point for students: the challenge of measuring the output of a production function for a service rather than for a good.

13.   A Cobb-Douglas function of the form $Q = aL^bK^{1-b}$ exhibits constant returns to scale. If the function is changed to $Q = aL^bk^c$, where b+c does not have to equal 1 (as it did in the former function), then the function can describe increasing returns to scale (if b+c>1) or decreasing returns to scale (if b+c<1).

14.   If b is less than 1, the production function exhibits diminishing marginal returns.

15.   True. In a Cobb-Douglas function with constant returns to scale, the sum of the coefficients is 1. Therefore, the coefficient of each input must be less than 1. A coefficient of less than one signifies decreasing marginal product to each input.

16. If Q = quantity produced and V is the quantity of the variable factor, then the equation $Q = bV - cV^2$ expresses a production function with diminishing marginal returns. Also, $Q = aV^b$ exhibits diminishing marginal returns as long as the exponent b is less than 1.

In order to show a production function with both increasing and decreasing returns, a cubic function is necessary:

$Q = bV + cV^2 - dV^3$.

PROBLEMS

1. a. FALSE   A firm's <u>marginal product</u> will start to <u>decrease</u>.

    b. TRUE   The increase in all of its inputs at an increasing rate will make up for the increase in output at a decreasing rate, thereby resulting in a constant rate of increase in output.

    c. TRUE   A linear short-run production function implies that output increases at a constant rate as the variable input is added to the production process.

    d. FALSE   Stage I ends shortly after this, when the already diminishing marginal product intersects the average product at the latter's maximum value.

2.

L	Q	MP	AP	MRP	W
0	0				
		50		175.00	
1	50		50.00		100
		60		210.00	
2	110		55.00		100
		190		665.00	
3	300		100.00		100
		150		525.00	
4	450		112.50		100
		140		490.00	
5	590		118.00		100
		75		262.50	
6	665		110.80		100
		35		122.50	
7	700		100.00		100
		25		87.50	
8	725		90.63		100
		-15		-52.50	
9	710		78.80		100

a. Based on the knowledge of the law of diminishing returns in relation to the three stages of production and without knowing the MP for the first three fishermen, we can surmise that the law of diminishing returns occurs with the addition of the fourth fisherman. This is because AP reaches its maximum at 5 fisherman and we know that the law of diminishing returns occurs just <u>before</u> this maximum is reached.

b. Stage I: 1 to 5 units of L
Stage II: 5 to 8 units of L
Stage III: 8 units of L and above

c. 7 L

d. They would have to drop one crew member from the boat and use only 6 fishermen. A decrease in the price of fish to $2.75 per pound cause the company to drop one crew member the boat and use only 6 fisherman. An increase in the market price of fish to $5.00 would make it economically feasible to hire the 8th fisherman.

e. Because the maximum catch in the short run for the boat is 725 pounds, the company would have to consider certain long-run actions. For example: 1) find more skilled fisherman 2) train the current crew to be more productive 3) seek out more abundant fishing areas 4) buy bigger or more modern boats 5) buy modern electronics equipment such as radar to find the fish more rapidly.

Instructors may ask students to think of other possibilities.

3. Based on the equation $Q = 50L + 6L^2 - .5L^3$, we can generate the following short run production schedule:

Variable Factor	Total Product	Average Product	Marginal Product
0	0.00		
1	55.50	55.50	55.50
2	120.00	60.00	64.50
3	190.50	63.50	70.50
4	264.00	66.00	73.50
5	337.50	67.50	73.50
6	408.00	68.00	70.50
7	472.50	67.50	64.50
8	528.00	66.00	55.50
9	571.50	63.50	43.50
10	600.00	60.00	28.50
11	610.50	55.50	10.50
12	600.00	50.00	-10.50
13	565.50	43.50	-34.50

(Please note that the marginal product in this schedule was calculated as the change in total product, as the variable factor is changed by one unit.)

a. The law of diminishing returns occurs at 4 units of input. Actually, the MP should be placed between each interval of input. Thus, the implication is that at 4 units, the marginal product is maximized. Instructors may wish to show this by asking students to find the derivative of marginal product (i.e., the second derivative of the total product function) setting it equal to zero and then solving for L.

$MP = 50 + 12L - 1.5L^2$

$dMP/dL = 12 - 3L = 0$

$L = 4$ (at the point where MP is maximized)

b. Stage I: 1 to 6 units of L
Stage II: 6 to 11 units of L
Stage III: 11 units of L and above

c. 9 workers. If the price drops to $7.50 the firm will have to consider reducing its labor force to only 8. In the long run, it would not have to change any of its fixed capacity, because it is still comfortably within Stage II of the production process.

4.

Vehicles	Mechanics	Total Cost*
100	2.5	$625,000
70	5.0	545,000
50	10.0	550,000
40	15.0	615,000
35	25.0	835,000
32	35.0	1,067,000

*There are obviously other costs involved in this operation. In this example, we are assuming that these two costs comprise the relevant costs for this decision.

a.   The use of 70 vehicles and 5 mechanics will minimize total cost.

b.

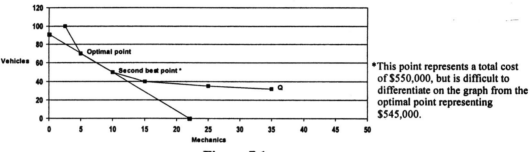

Figure 7.1

5.   a.   Mexico:

$$\frac{10}{1.5} = 6.67$$

Taiwan:

$$\frac{18}{3} = 6$$

Canada:

$$\frac{20}{6} = 3.33$$

It appears that Mexico is the best location because MP/P_L is the highest.

b.   Taiwan might be a better location than Mexico because its overhead is lower and its MP/P_L is very close to that of Mexico.

c.   Regardless of which location is chosen, the manufacturer should receive some advantages of economies of scale in the consolidation of its facilities. However, it will increase the risks associated with putting all of "its eggs in one basket."

Instructors may wish to discuss this further with the class. Possible risks: 1) passage of laws concerning environmental protection, trade, taxes etc.; 2) labor union issues; 3) relative changes in wage rates over time.

6.   a.

L	Q	MP	AP	MRP (P=$5)
0				
1	5.5	5.5	5.5	27.50
2	10.0	4.5	5.0	22.50
3	13.5	3.5	4.5	17.50
4	16.0	2.5	4.0	12.50
5	17.5	1.5	3.5	7.50
6	18.0	0.5	3.0	2.50
7	17.5	-0.5	2.5	-2.50

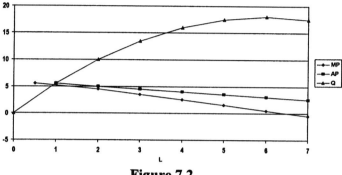

Figure 7.2

b.   5 workers

c.   No, because the 6th person has an MRP of $2.50. In order to hire this person, the wage rate would have to fall to at least this level.

7.   a. and b.

Variable Factor	Total Product	Average Product	Marginal Product
0	0.0		
1	7.5	7.5	7.5
2	15.6	7.8	8.1
3	23.7	7.9	8.1
4	31.2	7.8	7.5
5	37.5	7.5	6.3
6	42.0	7.0	4.5
7	44.1	6.3	2.1
8	43.2	5.4	-0.9
9	38.7	4.3	-4.5
10	30.0	3.0	-8.7

Note that the marginal product was calculated by finding the intervals between quantity for each addition of one variable factor. If the marginal product had been calculated as the first derivative of total product with respect to variable factor, the results would have been somewhat different.

c.

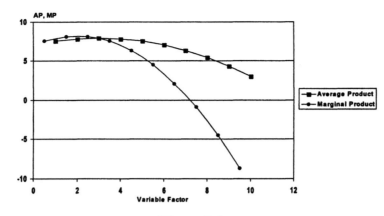

Figure 7.3

8.   a. and b.

Variable Factor	Total Product	Average Product	Marginal Product
0	0.0		6.5
1	6.5	6.5	5.5
2	12.0	6.0	4.5
3	16.5	5.5	3.5
4	20.0	5.0	2.5
5	22.5	4.5	1.5
6	24.0	4.0	0.5
7	24.5	3.5	-0.5
8	24.0	2.0	-1.5
9	22.5	2.5	-2.5
10	20.0	2.0	

The marginal product was calculated by the same method as in problem 2.

c.

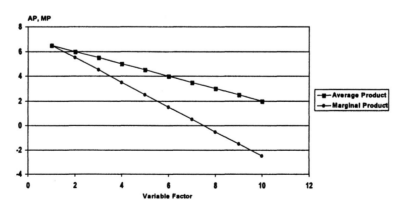

Figure 7.4

d.   The function in problem 7 was a cubic function, while in this problem it is a quadratic function. A cubic production function will show an area of increasing and then decreasing marginal product, while a quadratic function will show only the area of decreasing marginal product. The cubic function moves through all three stages of production, while a quadratic function covers only stages 2 and 3.

9. a. A regression was calculated for the observations given in the problem. The data were translated into logarithms and then a straight-line simple regression was computed. The result, in the log form of the equation is as follows:

$$\log Q = 1.889 + .414 \log M$$

The estimated quantities compared to the actuals (when anti-logs are taken) are:

Actual Quantity	Estimated Quantity
450	450
430	422
460	475
490	510
465	468
550	521
490	487

The coefficient of determination (R^2) is .84 and the t-test for the b-coefficient is 5.1.

b. The above results are fairly satisfactory. The coefficient of determination is relatively high, and the t-statistic for the slope coefficient is significant. The estimated results, shown above, are, in most instances, quite close to the actuals. Probably, some improvement could be obtained if a second variable input, such as utility bills, had been utilized as a second independent variable.

c. The formula for marginal product is bQ/M. The marginal products (based on estimated quantities) are shown below:

Materials	Estimated Quantity	Marginal Product
60	422	2.91
70	450	2.66
77	468	2.51
80	475	2.46
85	487	2.37
95	510	2.22
100	521	2.16

The results point to diminishing marginal product.

10. a. The regression which was calculated, a Cobb-Douglas function, was a power function, which when translated into logarithms converts to a straight-line regression. Thus,

$Q = aL^b K^c$ becomes
$\log Q = \log a + b(\log L) + c(\log K)$,

where Q = quantity, L = labor and K = capital.

When the regression was calculated (using a software package), these were the results:

$\log a = -.13489$ $R^2 = .98895$
$b = .825054$ t statistic for b = 2.522783
$c = .345781$ t statistic for c = 2.194156

The coefficient of determination, R^2 is very high, showing that most of the variation is explained by the regression equation. The two t-statistics are also sufficiently high to establish the b and c coefficients as statistically significant.

b.

Labor	Capital	Actual Quantity	Estimated Quantity
250	30	245	226.1
270	34	240	251.6
300	44	300	300.0
320	50	320	330.7
350	70	390	400.0
400	76	440	459.5
440	84	520	514.6
440	86	520	518.8
450	104	580	564.4
460	110	600	586.0
460	116	600	596.9

Based on the regression equation, estimated production is shown in the fourth column of the above table.

c. The sum of the two coefficients, b and c, is greater than 1 (.825 + .346 = 1.171). Therefore, the production function exhibits increasing returns to scale.

d. The elasticities of production of the two factors are their respective coefficients, b and c.

e. The marginal product of labor is decreasing since the coefficient b is less than 1.

11. a.

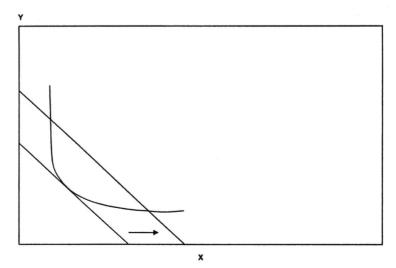

Figure 7.5

b.

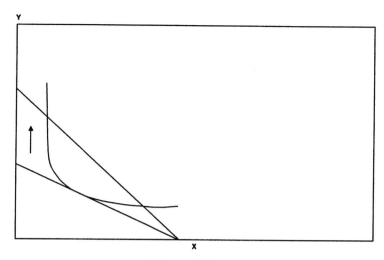

Figure 7.6

c.

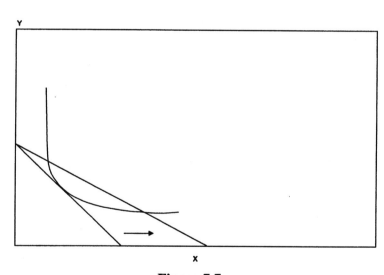

Figure 7.7

d.

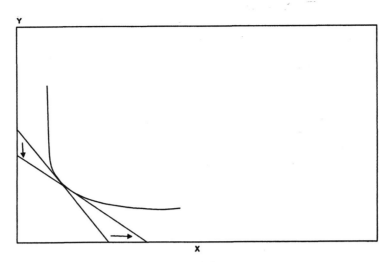

Figure 7.8

e.

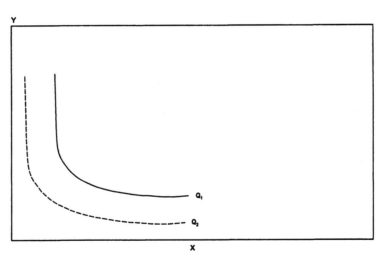

Figure 7.9

f.

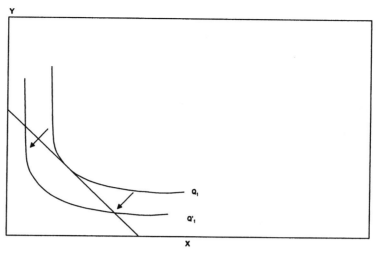

Figure 7.10

12. a. The numbers are the same as those in text Table 7B.1. This question gives an opportunity for students to see for themselves how this function can generate such numbers.

(Note to Instructors: Very often we have found that a simple exercise in "number crunching" helps students to really understand the nature of a mathematical function.)

  b. The isoquants can be easily identified by observations. Note that although some isoquants have only two combinations of output, they still qualify as such.

  c. This production function shows constant returns to scale.

13. a. CRTS

  b. CRTS

  c. IRTS

  d. DRTS

  e. IRTS

  f. IRTS

  g. For the Cobb-Douglas type of production function, the answers indicate that those whose coefficients sum to unity will exhibit CRTS, less that unity DRTS, and greater than unity IRTS. (Refer to problems 13a., b., c.)

Note: As a suggestion, students should try doubling each of the inputs and then determine what happens to output.

14. a. This is an IRTS production function.

   b. Because this function is expressed in the table an a discrete rather than continuous manner, there are two "optimal" input combinations instead of only one. They are:

   2Y and 6X   <u>or</u>   3Y and 4X.

   c. A decrease in the price of Y and an increase in the price of X will obviously cause the firm to use more Y and less X. That is, the firm will use either

   4Y and 3X   or   6Y and 2X.

   d.

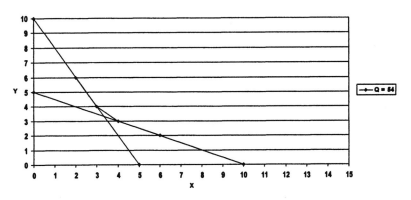

Figure 7.11

15. a. Since the coefficients add to more than one (.75+.3 = 1.05), this production function exhibits increasing returns to scale.

   b. | *Labor* | *Capital* | *Quantity* |
       | --- | --- | --- |
       | 100 | 0 | 132.9 |
       | 120 | 0 | 161.0 |
       | 150 | 75 | 203.5 |
       | 00 | 100 | 275.2 |
       | 00 | 150 | 421.3 |

   The existence of increasing returns to scale can be seen in the above table. For instance, the use of 150 units of labor and 75 units of capital is an increase of 50% over the use of 100 units of labor and 50 units of capital. The total product for the former (203.5 units) is 53% larger than the latter (132.9 units).

   c. With employment of 110 units of labor and 55 units of capital, the quantity produced will be 146.9 units compared to 132.9 units produced when labor is 100 and capital is 50. The change from 132.9 to 146.9 units represents an increase of 10.5%.

   d. If labor increases to 110 units from 100, while capital usage remains at 50, the quantity produced will be 142.8 units. This represents an increase of 7.4%.

The table below shows the total product when labor is increased by intervals of 10 but capital remains the same. The marginal product of labor is calculated at each point using the formula bQ/L.

Labor	Capital	Quantity	MP of Labor
100	50	132.9	.997
110	50	142.8	.974
120	50	152.4	.953
130	50	161.8	.934
140	50	171.1	.917
150	50	180.2	.901

The last column of the table shows that the marginal product of labor declines as more labor is added.

e. If capital were to increase by 10% from 50 to 55 while labor remains at 100, the quantity produced would increase to 136.8, an increase of about 2.9%.

f.

Labor	Capital	Quantity
100	50	105.6
120	60	126.7
150	75	158.4
200	100	211.2
300	150	316.8

Since the two coefficients now equal 1 (.7+.3=1), the situation is one of constant returns to scale. Thus, for instance, when labor is doubled from 150 to 300, and capital is doubled from 75 to 150, the quantity produced increases from 158.4 to 316.8 a precise doubling of total production.

CHAPTER 8 AND APPENDIXES
THE THEORY AND ESTIMATION OF COST

QUESTIONS

1. a. Sunk cost is a cost that is incurred in the past that is not affected by a current decision (except for purposes of taxes and possibly for the "full-cost" pricing of a product).

    Incremental cost is a cost that is affected by a current decision. It is measured by the change in cost relative to the change in a particular activity (e.g., construction of a new building, entry into the market with a new product, development of new software etc.)

    b. Fixed cost is a cost that does not vary with the level of business activity.

    Variable cost is a cost that does vary with the level of business activity.

    c. Incremental cost is the cost associated with a particular activity. Marginal cost is the per unit cost associated with a particular activity. For example, incremental cost is ΔTVC, while marginal cost is $\Delta TVC/\Delta Q$.

    d. Opportunity cost is the amount forgone when choosing one activity over the next best alternative. Out-of-pocket cost is the monetary cost associated with the choice of one activity over another. For example, the out-of-pocket cost of leaving one's job to attend school on a full-time basis is the tuition, books, etc. The opportunity cost is the loss of income from the job.

2. Incremental cost, variable cost, and marginal cost are considered "relevant costs" because the are affected by a current decision. Sunk cost is not considered relevant because it is incurred in the past and therefore not affected by a current decision. In the short run, fixed cost is also not considered to be relevant because a firm cannot change this amount regardless of its level of production or business activity. In contrast, incremental cost (and its per unit counterpart, marginal cost) and variable cost are considered to be relevant because they are affected by a current decision.

    Opportunity cost can also be considered a relevant cost, but it depends on the situation. For example, in the case of the decision to quit one's job to pursue an academic degree full time, the lost income from the job would be considered a relevant cost. However, suppose after one year of studies, the student considers quitting school (or attending school on a part-time basis) in order to return to work on a full-time basis. The lost income or opportunity cost of that one year in school would have to be considered "sunk."

3. The firm's short run cost function can be considered somewhat akin to a "mirror image" of its production function. As reflected in Figure 8.1 of the chapter, when its marginal product increases, its marginal cost decreases, and when its marginal product decreases (i.e., when the law of diminishing returns takes effect) its marginal cost starts to increase.

4. This statement is true. As indicated in the question above, the law of diminishing returns causes a firm's marginal cost to increase. This increase in marginal cost eventually causes a firm's average variable cost and average cost to increase.

5. From the standpoint of the supply side of the market, the short run is time enough only for those sellers already in the market to react to changes in the market by changing inputs (referred to as "variable inputs"). In the long run, firms may either enter or leave the market. Moreover, those firms already in the market have enough time to change all their production inputs.

6. Economies of scale is the decrease in a firm's unit cost of production as it increases all of its inputs (i.e., its "scale" of production). Economies of scale can be considered the monetary equivalent of increasing returns to scale. That is, when a firm's output increases by a greater proportion than the increase in its inputs, its unit cost of production decreases.

    The main determinants of economies of scale are summarized in Table 8.4 of the chapter. Instructors may wish to divide these factors into the "financial" and the "real." The financial factors are: a)productive capacity of certain capital equipment rises faster than purchase price b)discounts from bulk purchases c)lower cost of raising capital funds. The other factors listed in the Table can be considered real factors because they relate primarily to the nature of the production process.

7. Diseconomies of scale is the increase in a firm's unit cost of production as it increases all of its inputs. The main determinants of diseconomies of scale are also listed in Table 8.4. Perhaps the most important of these factors are a)management coordination and control problems and b)the disproportionate rise in staff and indirect labor.

8. Economies of scope refers to the reduction in unit cost resulting from a firm's production of two or more products. This type of cost savings is related to economies of scale to the extent that a firm of a larger size is more likely to produce a variety of goods, thereby increasing the probability of experiencing economies of scope. However, economies of scale does not necessarily lead to economies of scope and economies of scope does not depend on the existence of scale economies.

9. The learning curve indicates unit costs on the basis of an accumulation of output. The typical cost function indicates unit cost associated with different levels of output in a given time period. In other words, the cost function is not cumulative. Because the learning curve was not considered explicitly in the neo-classical theory of the firm, we can only suggest that the learning curve phenomenon is more consistent with the long run. This is because, in the short run, we are assuming a certain level of skills, technology, etc. and are also assuming that the firm is using them to the best of their ability (i.e., is operating somewhere on the cost line, whatever the level of output).

10. As explained in the text, the experience curve is often considered synonymous with the learning curve. However, certain people prefer to consider it in a broader context. The introduction of either the learning curve or the experience curve phenomenon would cause a downward shift in the firm's unit cost curves.

11. After reading the section "The Long-Run Average Cost Curve as the Envelope of Short-Run Average Cost," students should agree with this statement. As seen in Figure 8.9, for the output level marked by the asterisk on unit cost curve "B," the firm would be incurring a lower unit cost by using the larger capacity "C" rather than using the smaller capacity "B" at its most efficient point. This is because the economies of scale made possible by the larger capacity more than makes up for the fact the this larger capacity is not being run at its point of minimum unit cost.

12. Accounting statements, as a rule, do not differentiate between costs and expenses which are relevant to decision making and those that are not. Included in cost of goods sold can be such items as fixed overhead and depreciation which is time-related (and not production-related). Thus, not all costs included in cost of goods sold are relevant according to the economist's definition. Many of

the expenses included in selling, administrative and general, and research and development expenses are fixed, and thus not relevant to decision making. However, there are expenses which vary with quantities. Commissions paid to sales representatives would be an example. Other types of selling and advertising expenses can also be quantity-related, and thus would be relevant to decision making.

13. This person is referring to the spreading out of fixed cost in as short-run situation. Economies of scale is more properly used in a long-run situation in which all inputs can be changed.

14. In the economic short-run, at least one factor remains fixed. In estimating such cost functions, economists assume that capital is fixed while labor is the variable factor. Thus, the data used in this regression analysis must cover observations where quantities produced and costs change while certain factors remain unchanged. The method usually selected is the time-series technique over a period of time. This time period must supply enough observations so that production and cost changes can be observed while the size of plant and its technology remain relatively unchanged. Thus the time period should not be too long—for instance, twenty-four to thirty-six monthly observations, or possibly 52 weekly observations.

Some of the problems encountered and for which adjustments must be sought are the following:

a. Prices of labor, materials and other variable factors may change over the time period, and must be adjusted to be consistent.

b. Cost should include only those which vary with quantity produced.

c. Accounting data are usually employed in cost estimation. Economists would prefer economic costs. If it is possible to include opportunity costs, adjustments of this kind should be made.

d. If there are changes in tax rates, social security contributions, or other similar costs, adjustments should be made to make them comparable over time.

e. If there has been a change in accounting methods during the period of the study, such change must be adjusted to obtain consistency in the data.

f. Some actual cash outlays may be incurred at discrete intervals and recorded as costs at that time. However, the actual costs are incurred continuously. Overhauls and maintenance are examples. Such costs should be spread over the period in which they are incurred.

15. In the economic long run, there are no fixed costs. The economist usually assumes that changes in the size of plant can occur. So, the regression method generally used is the cross-sectional analysis, where observations on output and costs are taken from different plants at one point of time.

The problems which will be encountered in this analysis and some of the adjustments which may have to be made are:

a.   Wage rates and other unit costs (e.g. utility bills) may vary from one geographical area to another. Such differences must be adjusted to make these costs consistent from area to area.

b.   The various plants may not be operating at an optimal level of technology. Plants in the sample should be carefully selected to include plants which are relatively homogeneous.

c.   If the different plants in the sample belong to a different firm, there may be differences in accounting methods, and such differences will have to be adjusted, if possible, to make the data consistent.

d.   Some factors, especially labor, may receive their remuneration differently. For instance, vacation times may differ, or some pay may be in the form of company stock, etc. Again, such differences must be investigated and, where possible, adjusted for consistency.

13.   a.   Engineering costs: based on data developed by experts (engineers), who estimate the optimal quantity of inputs needed to produce various quantities of outputs. The inputs are then costed, and total cost for each output is established. Advantages of this method include keeping technology and output mix constant and avoiding problems caused by inflation. However, the estimates are based on what experts expect them to be, and are not based on actual (historical) data. Associated costs may be omitted. Further, the calculations are based on ideal circumstances and may not consider actual production situations.

b.   Survivorship principle: Plants in an industry are categorized by size, and the proportion of total industry output for each size class is calculated. These computations are repeated over an interval of several years. Then, if a particular size category appears to grow relative to others, it is concluded that it is more efficient than the others. A long run cost curve can be determined from these observations. A major advantage of this method is that reliance on accounting cost data (and their necessary adjustments) is eliminated. Also, it is a relatively simple method to implement. However, it tells us nothing about actual cost levels; it does not recognize industry changes due to technological advances; it implicitly assumes that competitive circumstances (i.e. cost levels) determine survival rather than industry practices which may not be consistent with competition.

PROBLEMS

1.

Q	TC	TFC	TVC	AC	AF	AVC	MC
0	120	120	0	X	X	X	
1	265	120	145	265	120	145	145
2	384	120	264	192	60	132	119
3	483	120	363	161	40	121	99
4	568	120	448	142	30	112	85
5	645	120	525	129	24	105	77
6	720	120	600	120	20	100	75
7	799	120	679	114.1	17.1	97	79
8	888	120	768	111	15	96	89
9	993	120	873	110.3	13.3	97	105
10	1120	120	1000	112	12	100	127

2. Although the numbers are fictitious, this problem is actually based on a study conducted by one of the authors. (See Philip K. Y. Young, "Family Labor, Sacrifice, and Competition: The Case of Korean Greengrocers in New York City," *Amerasia: The Journal of Asian American Studies*, UCLA, Fall/Winter 1983. Mr. Lee's opportunity cost of taking the job with the chemical firm is his foregone store profits before taxes of $175,000.)

However, in return Mr. Lee will receive the following:

Salary plus benefits	$95,000
Net rent ($50,000 minus taxes, insurance, etc., of $300,000)	20,000
Interest income (9% of $300,000)	27,000
Total	$142,000

On the surface, it could be argued that the benefit of taking the job is not sufficient to offset the opportunity cost of giving up his own business. However consider the points below.

a. The long hours of work reduces the attractiveness of owning one's own business.

b. The profits have to be shared with his wife and brother. If he takes the job, his wife and brother may then decide to get their own jobs.

c. Although the forecast is that the profits in his own business and his salary will increase at the same rate in the future, each involves its own risks. A downturn in the economy or increasing competition (particularly from other Koreans who open up their own stores) may sharply reduce profits. On the other hand, working for someone else entails the risk of being laid off.

Finally, there is always the argument of the "psychic benefits" that one receives by being his or her own boss. Instructors may wish to discuss this further, particularly in light of the extremely long hours that one work in owning and operating a business.

3. Instructors should have an interesting time discussing this question. We recommend that this question be answered in class by small groups of students (perhaps 4 to 6). Each group should be allowed a short time to discuss the problem and to reach a consensus about the cost estimate. We

have found that it is extremely rare for two groups to arrive at the same estimate. We have also found that groups may not be able to agree upon a single estimate.

There is no unique answer to this question because it all depends on the assumptions that one makes about the cost conditions. However, based on the strict criteria of relevant cost (i.e. incremental or variable cost), we suggest that the following estimate:

Boat fuel	$45
Travel expenses (gas, oil, and tires only)	18
Bait, etc.	50
Food	40
Beverages	35
	$188 or $9.40 per fish

Of course, it can also be argued that a certain amount of the food and beverage costs should not be included because he would incur these costs regardless of whether he goes fishing. Also, at the risk of stirring up a heated debate, instructors may also wish to consider the opportunity cost of Sarah's time in cleaning the fish (and in fact why she has to clean the fish in the first place!)

4.   a.

Quantity	Average Variable Cost	Average Total Cost	Marginal Cost
0			
1	57.10	157.10	57.10
2	54.40	104.40	51.70
3	51.90	85.23	46.90
4	49.60	74.60	42.70
5	47.50	67.50	39.10
6	45.60	62.27	36.10
7	43.90	58.19	33.70
8	42.40	54.90	31.90
9	41.10	52.21	30.70
10	40.00	50.00	30.10
11	39.10	48.19	30.10
12	38.40	46.73	30.70
13	37.90	45.59	31.90
14	37.60	44.74	33.70
15	37.50	44.17	36.10
16	37.60	43.85	39.10
17	37.90	43.78	42.70
18	38.40	43.96	46.90
19	39.10	44.36	51.70
20	40.00	45.00	57.10

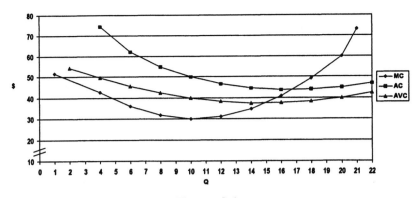

Figure 8.1

Quantity	Average Variable Cost	Average Total Cost	Marginal Cost
0			
1	63.00	163.00	63.00
2	66.00	116.00	69.00
3	69.00	102.33	75.00
4	72.00	97.00	81.00
5	75.00	95.00	87.00
6	78.00	94.67	93.00
7	81.00	95.29	99.00
8	84.00	96.50	105.00
9	87.00	98.11	111.00
10	90.00	100.00	117.00
11	93.00	102.09	123.00
12	96.00	104.33	129.00
13	99.00	106.69	135.00
14	102.00	109.14	141.00
15	105.00	111.67	147.00
16	108.00	114.25	153.00
17	111.00	116.88	159.00
18	114.00	119.56	165.00
19	117.00	122.26	171.00
20	120.00	125.00	177.00

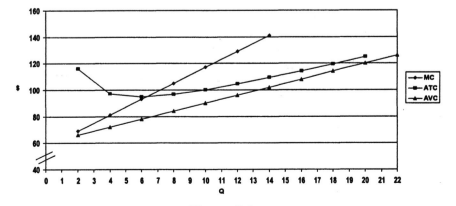

Figure 8.2

Quantity	Average Variable Cost	Average Total Cost	Marginal Cost
0			
1	60.00	160.00	60.00
2	60.00	110.00	60.00
3	60.00	93.33	60.00
4	60.00	85.00	60.00
5	60.00	80.00	60.00
6	60.00	76.67	60.00
7	60.00	74.29	60.00
8	60.00	72.50	60.00
9	60.00	71.11	60.00
10	60.00	70.00	60.00
11	60.00	69.09	60.00
12	60.00	68.33	60.00
13	60.00	67.69	60.00
14	60.00	67.14	60.00
15	60.00	66.67	60.00
16	60.00	66.25	60.00
17	60.00	65.88	60.00
18	60.00	65.56	60.00
19	60.00	65.26	60.00
20	60.00	65.00	60.00

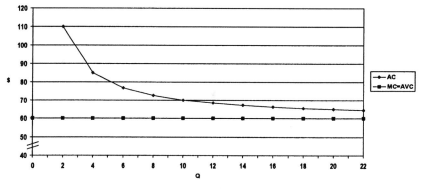

Figure 8.3

b. In the first equation, diminishing returns occurs at 10 units of output, the point at which MC reaches its minimum point.

In the second equation, diminishing returns begins immediately after production starts.

In the third equation, diminishing returns does not occur over the range of output being considered.

In the first and second equations, the point of minimum average cost occurs at the point at which MC intersects the AC curve (i.e. approximately 17 and 6, respectively). The minimum point is never actually reached in the case of the third equation.

c. Students should simply observe how the MC intersects the AVC and AC lines at their minimum points in the cubic equation; how MC is always above AVC in the quadratic equation, and how MC is actually equal to AVC and never quite intersects the AC line in the case of the linear equation.

5. a. FALSE   Decision-makers should always use the replacement or current cost of raw materials because it is considered to be relevant to the decision.

    b. TRUE   The mathematical relationship between the marginal and average assures that this will always be the case.

    c. TRUE   Declining average cost indicates economies of scale and increasing average cost indicates diseconomies of scale.

    d. FALSE   Marginal cost is also considered in the long run cost structure. See Table 8.3 and Figure 8.5 in text.

    e. FALSE   The rational firm will try to operate most efficiently by making sure that its unit costs are exactly as indicated by its cost structure (i.e. as seen by observing any of the points on its average cost curve).

6. a. Only AC will shift downwards, because we assume that this move affects only fixed cost.

    b. This will cause a leftward movement along the AC and AVC curves.

    c. This should not change either the AC or the AVC curves.

    d. This should shift AC and AVC downwards.

    e. This should cause the AC and AVC curves to shift upwards.

7. a. LRAC = 160 - 20Q + 1.2Q2
        LRMC = 160 - 40Q + 3.6Q^2

    b. Because of the particular functional form of the LRAC, we know that this firm experiences economies of scale at about 8 units of output (8.3 to be exact). Beyond this, it experiences diseconomies of scale. See the diagram below.

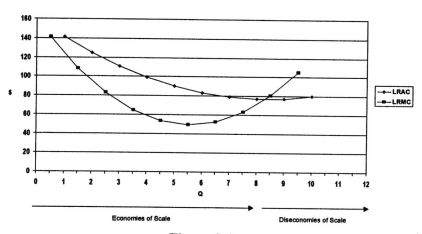

Figure 8.4

8. a. This equation represents a quadratic cost curve. Total fuel cost (Y) is the dependent variable and quantity produced (X) is the independent variable. Since the cost function includes a positive squared term, marginal costs are increasing. The average variable cost curve is also increasing, while the total cost curve (which includes a fixed element, 16.68) probably exhibits a u-shape. The total cost curve rises at an increasing rate. Since the observations were taken for one plant over a period of time, time-series regression analysis was used.

    b. This is a time-series analysis of the steel industry. The total cost equation shown is a straight line. The marginal and average variable cost curves are horizontal, i.e. costs are constant. If $182.1 million is assumed to be fixed cost, then the average total cost curve will be declining. A twelve-year period is probably too long a period over which to assume that plant sizes and technology remained unchanged.

9. a.

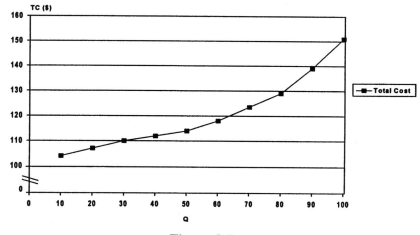

Figure 8.5

The total cost function appears to be a cubic function.

b.-c. The following three formulas were used:

Straight line: TC = a + bQ
Regression: TC = 94.9333 + .4603Q
R^2 = .909
t-statistic for b: 8.96

Quadratic: TC = a + bQ + cQ²
Regression: TC = 106.6833 - .1272Q + .0053Q²
R2 = .988
t-statistic   a: -1.413
                    b: 6.697

Cubic: TC = a + bQ - cQ² + dQ³
Regression: TC = 99.5 +.5099Q - .0085Q² + .000083Q³
R2 = .999
t-statistic   a: 6.30
                    b: -5.072
                    c: 8.357

The cubic function appears to give the best fit; it has the highest coefficient of determination, and all the t-statistics are significant. The signs of the coefficients (all positive except the coefficient of Q²) are correct.

d. Yes. Time series analysis is usually employed for short-run cost studies.

e. If the data represented observations for 10 different plants at the same point in time, then the regression analysis would have been cross-sectional. Cross-section regression analysis is ordinarily employed for the estimation of long run cost functions.

10. The following table represents all the relevant cost data for quantities 1 to 10. It has been assumed that the constant term in the equation (equaling 50) represents fixed cost. Marginal costs have been calculated as the differences in total cost as one unit of quantity is added (rather than using calculus. The interested student can make this calculation).

Quantity	Total Fixed Cost	Total Variable Cost	Average Total Cost	Average Fixed Cost	Variable Cost	Total Cost	Marginal Cost
0	50	0.00	50.00				
1	50	14.20	64.20	50.00	14.20	64.20	14.20
2	50	26.60	75.60	25.00	12.80	37.80	11.40
3	50	35.40	85.40	16.67	11.80	28.47	9.80
4	50	44.80	94.80	12.50	11.20	23.70	9.40
5	50	55.00	105.00	10.00	11.00	21.00	10.20
6	50	67.20	117.20	8.33	11.20	19.53	12.20
7	50	82.60	132.60	7.14	11.80	18.94	15.40
8	50	102.40	152.40	6.25	12.80	19.05	19.80
9	50	127.80	177.80	5.56	14.20	19.76	25.40
10	50	160.00	210.00	5.00	16.00	21.00	32.20

a.

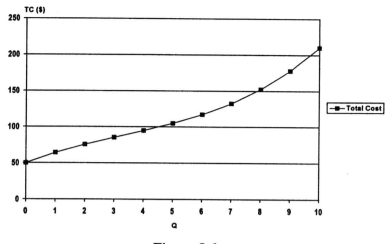

Figure 8.6

b.   All data are shown in the table above.

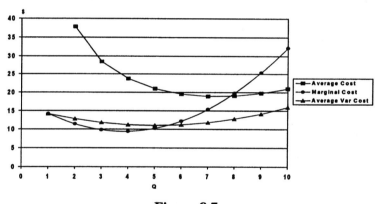

Figure 8.7

c.   Grand Corporation has a cubic cost function. This means that it passes through all three cost areas. Looking at the marginal cost curve, decreasing marginal costs prevail until 4 units are produced, after which increasing marginal costs are present. As the marginal cost passes from decreasing to increasing, it arrives at a minimum point at which it is constant.

11. a.   (1) $TC = 20 + 4Q$

Quantity	Total Fixed Cost	Total Variable Cost	Total Cost	Average Fixed Cost	Average Variable Cost	Average Total Cost	Marginal Cost
0	20	0.00	20.00				
1	20	4.00	24.00	20.00	4.00	24.00	4.00
2	20	8.00	28.00	10.00	4.00	14.00	4.00
3	20	12.00	32.00	6.67	4.00	10.67	4.00
4	20	16.00	36.00	5.00	4.00	9.00	4.00
5	20	20.00	40.00	4.00	4.00	8.00	4.00
6	20	24.00	44.00	3.33	4.00	7.33	4.00
7	20	28.00	48.00	2.86	4.00	6.86	4.00
8	20	32.00	52.00	2.50	4.00	6.50	4.00
9	20	36.00	56.00	2.22	4.00	6.22	4.00
10	20	40.00	60.00	2.00	4.00	6.00	4.00

(2) $TC = 20 + 2Q + .5Q^2$

Quantity	Total Fixed Cost	Total Variable Cost	Total Cost	Average Fixed Cost	Average Variable Cost	Average Total Cost	Marginal Cost
0	20	0.00	20.00				
1	20	2.50	22.50	20.00	2.50	22.50	2.50
2	20	6.00	26.00	10.00	3.00	13.00	3.50
3	20	10.50	30.50	6.67	3.50	10.17	4.50
4	20	16.00	36.00	5.00	4.00	9.00	5.50
5	20	22.50	42.50	4.00	4.50	8.50	6.50
6	20	30.00	50.00	3.33	5.00	8.33	7.50
7	20	38.50	58.50	2.86	5.50	8.36	8.50
8	20	48.00	68.00	2.50	6.00	8.50	9.50
9	20	58.50	78.50	2.22	6.50	8.72	10.50
10	20	70.00	90.00	2.00	7.00	9.00	11.50

(3) $TC = 20 + 4Q - .1Q^2$

Quantity	Total Fixed Cost	Total Variable Cost	Total Cost	Average Fixed Cost	Average Variable Cost	Average Total Cost	Marginal Cost
0	20	0.00	20.00				
1	20	3.90	23.90	20.00	3.90	23.90	3.90
2	20	7.60	27.60	10.00	3.80	13.80	3.70
3	20	11.10	31.10	6.67	3.70	10.37	3.50
4	20	14.40	34.40	5.00	3.60	8.60	3.30
5	20	17.50	37.50	4.00	3.50	7.50	3.10
6	20	20.40	40.40	3.33	3.40	6.73	2.90
7	20	23.10	43.10	2.86	3.30	6.16	2.70
8	20	25.60	45.60	2.50	3.20	5.70	2.50
9	20	27.90	47.90	2.22	3.10	5.32	2.30
10	20	30.00	50.00	2.00	3.00	5.00	2.10

b.

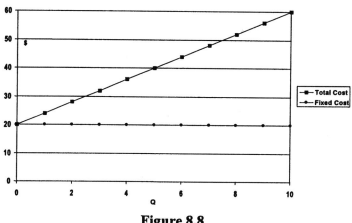

Figure 8.8

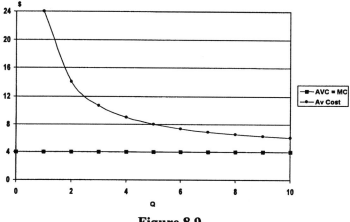

Figure 8.9

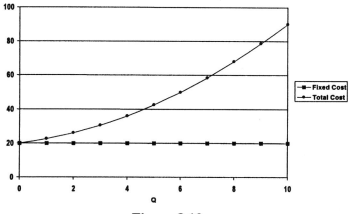

Figure 8.10

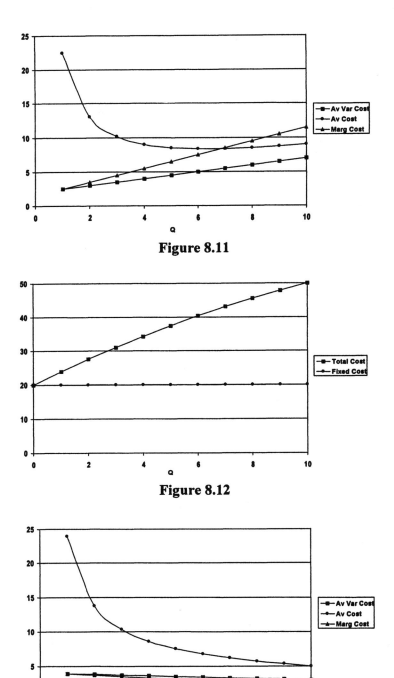

Figure 8.11

Figure 8.12

Figure 8.13

c. We have assumed that the first term on the right side of the equation (20) represents fixed costs.

Cost function (1) is a straight line function. There are no increasing marginal costs. Marginal cost and average variable costs are constant and equal to each other.

Cost function (2) exhibits increasing marginal costs, and the total cost increases at an increasing rate.

Cost function (3) shows a total cost curve which increases at a decreasing rate. Marginal cost and average costs decrease throughout the range.

10. a. Variable costs:

Paper stock		8000	
Printing		50000	
Binding		22000	
Shipping		10000	
Total		90000	
Total per unit (/10000)			9.00
Royalty per unit	0.13	48	6.24
Commission per unit	0.03	48	1.44
Variable cost per unit			16.68

Fixed costs:

Typesetting	15000
Art	9000
Editing	20000
Reviews	3000
Promotion and advertising	12000
Total fixed cost	59000

Quantity	Fixed Cost	Variable Cost	Total Cost	Average Total Cost	Average Variable Cost	Marginal Cost
0	59000	0	59000			
2000	59000	33360	92360	46.18	16.68	16.68
4000	59000	66720	125720	31.43	16.68	16.68
6000	59000	100080	159080	26.51	16.68	16.68
8000	59000	133440	192440	24.06	16.68	16.68
10000	59000	166800	225800	22.58	16.68	16.68
12000	59000	200160	259160	21.60	16.68	16.68
14000	59000	233520	292520	20.89	16.68	16.68
16000	59000	266880	325880	20.37	16.68	16.68
18000	59000	300240	359240	19.96	16.68	16.68
20000	59000	333600	392600	19.63	16.68	16.68

Total Cost = 59000 + 16.68Q
Average Total Cost = 59000/Q + 16.68
Average Variable Cost = 16.68
Marginal Cost = 16.68

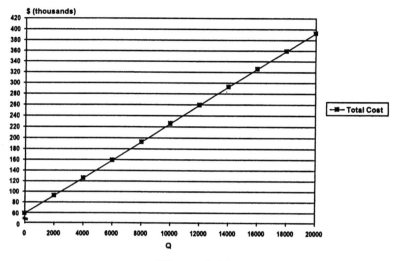

Figure 8.14

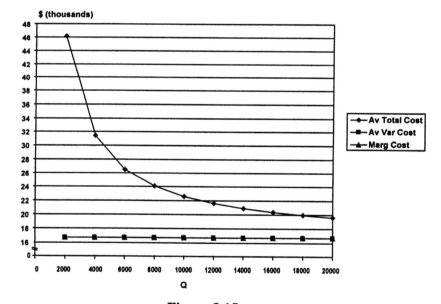

Figure 8.15

11.   a.

Quantity	Total Cost	Average Total Cost	Average Variable Cost	Marginal Cost
0	170.0			
1	193.5	193.50	23.50	23.50
2	220.0	110.00	25.00	26.50
3	249.5	83.17	26.50	29.50
4	282.0	70.50	28.00	32.50
5	317.5	63.50	29.50	35.50
6	356.0	59.33	31.00	38.50
7	397.5	56.79	32.50	41.50
8	442.0	55.25	34.00	44.50
9	489.5	54.39	35.50	47.50
10	540.0	54.00	37.00	50.50
11	593.5	53.95	38.50	53.50
12	650.0	54.17	40.00	56.50
13	709.5	54.58	41.50	59.50
14	772.0	55.14	43.00	62.50
15	837.5	55.83	44.50	65.50

b.

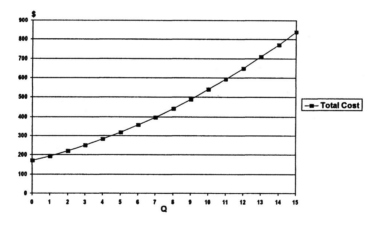

Figure 8.16

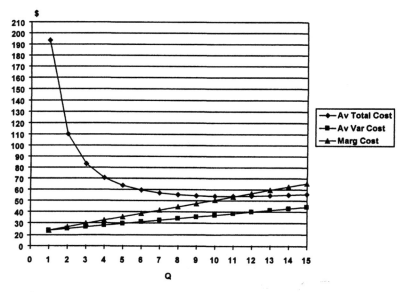

Figure 8.17

c. Big Horn's cost curves do not include decreasing and constant marginal costs. As can be seen from above graphs, the marginal cost curve rises from the first unit produced.

CHAPTER 9
PRICING AND OUTPUT DECISIONS:
PERFECT COMPETITION AND MONOPOLY

QUESTIONS

1. All four of the characteristics listed in Figure 9.1 of Chapter 9 are important to ensuring that buyers and sellers are price takers. Students should recognize that the absence of any one of these factors could enable market participants to exercise a certain degree of market power. Let us consider each factor from the standpoint of sellers.

   a. Large number of relatively small sellers: This factor provides buyers with a considerable number of easily available alternatives. If one seller tries to raise its price, consumers can turn to the many others who would be willing to sell a product at the going market price. The relatively small size of a seller would tend to constrain any individual seller from lowering its price. After all, if its relatively small size enables it to sell all it wants to at the going market price, why rock the boat?

   b. Standardized product: This ensures that the many alternative sellers mentioned above are perceived by consumers to be exactly the same as the one which tried to raise the price. If this particular firm succeeded in convincing consumers that its product was "better," it might be able to get people to buy the product at the higher price.

   c. Complete information about market price: One of the many small sellers could get away with charging a higher price if consumers were ignorant about the lower priced alternatives. Complete information by all consumers prevents this from happening.

   d. Freedom of entry and exit: This prevents any possibility of sellers exercising some degree of market power <u>in the long run</u>. As illustrated in the chapter, if the price of a product rises because demand has increased, the long run entry of new sellers will tend to push the price back down. If the entry of newcomers is interfered with, those sellers already in the market would enjoy "monopolistic" profits.

2. This question is answered in 1.d. above.

3. Although there are very few "perfectly competitive" markets, the basic short run and long run behavior hypothesized by the perfectly competitive model can be found in all types of market structures in the "market economy." Thus, managers would be well advised to learn about all types of markets, including perfect competition. The popular press is filled with stories of companies who either succeed or fail in following the behavior predicted by the perfectly competitive model. For example, looking at the personal computer market over the past decade, we can see a general pattern of change very similar to the perfectly competitive model (although the details do not quite fit).

   a. The increase in demand caused an increase in profits of those selling the product.

   b. This prompted the entry of many new sellers, including IBM. (At one point in the early 1980s, we recall one PC magazine listing over 100 manufacturers of PCs.)

c.   The increase in supply (particularly by the direct marketing "800 number" companies such as Dell and Northgate) caused prices to fall, leading to an industry "shakeout."

Instructors may want to expand this point by discussing the factors that were more related the characteristics on non-perfectly competitive markets. For example: IBM's entry into the PC market turning the market (at least temporarily) into more of an oligopoly, IBM's replacement of its "AT" type computer with its PS/2 line of computers as an attempt to differentiate itself from its competitors and thereby maintain some degree of market power.

4.   From the standpoint of an individual, price-taking firm in a perfectly competitive market, the demand is <u>perceived</u> to be perfectly elastic because it can sell as much as—or as little as—it wants to at the going market price.

5.   The more alternatives (or substitute products) available for consumers, the more sensitive they will be to a change in the price of a product sold by a particular seller.

6.   a.   According to economic theory, new firms enter the market when they see that firms already in the market are earning economic profit. Thus, for firms already in the market, there is a proverbial "goods news/bad news" situation. Good news: it is earning economic profit. Bad news: things are going to get a lot rougher as new competitors enter the market.

b.   We believe that there is much truth in this statement. One of the risks that an entrepreneur takes is to commit his or her firm's resources to a particular product or service on the promise of future growth and profitability (i.e., due to an increase in demand) rather than current profitability. However, the two roles are not necessarily mutually exclusive. One could be an "entrepreneurial manager" by going into a market because of the anticipation of demand increases even though the "MR=MC" rule indicates a loss or only normal profit.

7.   P>AVC is the per unit version of TR>TVC. When TR>TVC, the firm is earning a positive contribution margin.

8.   "Normal" is akin to equilibrium in economic theory. When a firm earns a profit (i.e., a non-zero profit), a disequilibrium situation would result as firms start to enter the market, driving down the price and forcing all firms into a situation in which they can earn no profit above zero.

9.   A popular measure of financial performance being used by an increasing number of American firms is "economic value added" or EVA. This term is defined as operating profit minus taxes minus the firm's cost of capital. The idea is that if the firm's EVA is positive, it is helping to "create value" for its shareholders. A positive EVA is very similar in concept to the "economic profit" of microeconomic theory.

10. Perfectly competitive firms are price takers. This means that they can sell as much or as little as they want, but only at the going market price. When this happens, the market price is the same as their marginal revenue. Thus, P=MC is the same as P=MR.

11. Revenue is maximized when marginal revenue becomes zero. Profit is maximized when MR = MC. If marginal cost is positive, then the profit maximizing price will be higher than the revenue maximizing price. The price at which revenue is maximized will, therefore, be lower than the profit maximizing price.

12. Here are three examples:

   (1) Intel: Should we go into the "data farm"(or "farm business")? In mid 1999, they said yes.
   (2) In 1999, IBM decided to drop the production of networking hardware and become a sales and distribution arm of Cisco.
   (3) In 1999, Motorola divested its semiconductor business (sold to managers in a leveraged buyout deal).

13. All the markets with the exception of the oil market would be considered pretty close to if not exactly like the "perfectly competitive" market. OPEC still has some degree of market power in the oil market, although not as much as before. Some would argue that large institutional traders have the power to affect the stock market price, particularly in certain stocks.

14. Because of the long approval cycle for a new drug (up to 10 years) and the high cost, the patent helps to reward drug companies with the possibility of earning economic profit over the life of the patent.

PROBLEMS

1.   Given the market price and its cost structure, this firm will be incurring a loss. However, this loss will not be as large as its fixed cost. In other words, this firm will have a positive contribution margin. In the short run, it should remain in operation. In the long run, it may have to consider dropping out of this market if the price does not rise above its average cost or if it cannot manage to lower its average cost below the market price. However, other firms may decide to drop out before it does and their actions may cause the market price to rise (i.e., a long run leftward shift in supply). Furthermore, for some reason, demand may increase in the long run, thereby causing price to rise (i.e., a long run rightward shift in demand).

2.   a. FALSE   Not if its loss is less than its fixed cost. See explanation of problem 1.

      b. FALSE   Even a pure monopoly has to consider the possibility of demand falling below the level sufficient to earn a profit. (For example, even if Polaroid continues to have a monopoly on cameras that use instant developing film, can they stop the erosion in demand due to the one-hour photo developing machines and cameras that record images electronically on discs?)

      c. TRUE   Other factors held constant, the entry or exit of firms will theoretically lead to this condition.

      d. TRUE   In order to maximize revenue, a firm will price its product at the point where MR=0. By implication, this must be a lower price than the point where MR=MC.

      e. TRUE   If P>AVC but P<AC, then the company will cover some of its fixed costs; thus, loss will be less than fixed cost.

      f. FALSE   Price will be more than MR.

      g. FALSE   This depends on the demand for its product. The demand curve can shift to the left. While a monopoly may earn profits in the short run, the long run monopoly profits are often eroded as competition and changes in technology make monopolies vulnerable.

3.   a. Because Kelson's marginal cost function is linear, it implies that its total cost function is quadratic. This indicates that the law of diminishing returns takes effect as soon as production begins.

      b. At Q = 1500, MC = \$157.50
          At Q = 2000, MC = \$160.00
          At Q = 3500, MC = \$167.50

      c. MC = \$150 + 0.005Q = \$175
          $Q^* = 5000$

      d. The supply curve is essentially the portion of a firm's marginal cost curve above its average variable cost (i.e., the shut down point). Although fixed and variable cost is not provided, we can assume that over a certain range, the firm is earning either a profit or is incurring a loss greater than its fixed cost. Thus, the following is a suggested short run supply schedule:

P	Q
$175	5000
180	6000
185	7000
190	8000
etc.	

4. a.

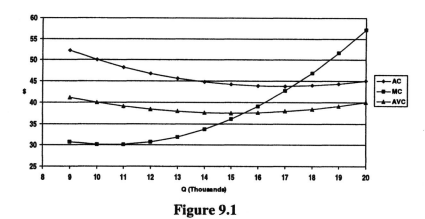

Figure 9.1

b. Yes. If P = $50, the firm should produce 18 units and earn an economic profit of $108.72.

c. If P = $35, then the best that the firm could do by operating would be to produce 14 units (i.e., by following the MR=MC rule). However, this would cause it to lose $136.36, a sum greater than the implied fixed cost of $99.96 (rounded to $100). Thus the firm should shut down.

5. a. P* = $1090.

b. The above price would enable a firm to earn a maximum amount of total profit in the short run. However, it may want to consider charging a higher price if it wanted to position its product as a "premium" product. It might also want to set a higher price if it suspected that future competition would eventually force all competitors to lower their price. Without more specific data about these other considerations, it would be difficult to suggest a specific price that is higher than $1090. As a generalization, we can only say that the firm would set a higher price if it gives greater priority to goals mentioned above.

c. The firm would want to consider setting a price lower than $1090 if it wanted to increase its revenue (i.e., market share). As can be seen in the numerical example, if the firm charged $850, its total revenue would be $850,000 (as compared to $763,000 at the price of $1090). In fact, it could continue lowering its price in order to increase its revenue up to the point at which MR=0 (not shown in the table).

There may be other reasons for lowering the price. For example, the firm may wish to use the strategy of "learning curve pricing" (see Chapter 8). It may also choose to be an aggressive price-cutter in an oligopolistic market.

6. a. To solve this problem, we find the MR and MC functions, set them equal to each other, and solve for the optimal Q. Using this Q, we then find the optimal P.

P = 853.37 - 0.06Q
TR = 853.37Q - 0.06Q^2
MR = 853.37 - 0.12Q

MC = 0.85 + 0.03Q

853.37 - 0.12Q = .85 + 0.03Q

Q* = 5683.466
P = 853.37 - 0.06(5683.466)
P* = $512.36

This price can then be rounded to a more even number (e.g., $500).

b.

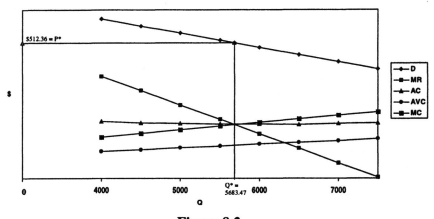

Figure 9.2

7.   a.   To answer this question, we illustrate how Excel software can help to answer this question. Using the online software provided for users of this text, we arrive at the following:

Quantity	Price	Total Revenue	Total Fixed Cost	Total Variable Cost	Total Cost	Total Profit
0	100	0	50	0	50.00	-50.00
1	92	92	50	71	120.60	-28.60
2	84	168	50	125	174.80	-6.80
3	76	228	50	166	216.20	11.80
4	68	272	50	198	248.40	23.60
5	60	300	50	225	275.00	25.00
6	52	312	50	250	299.60	12.40
7	44	308	50	276	325.80	-17.80
8	36	288	50	307	357.20	-69.20
9	28	252	50	347	397.40	-145.40
10	20	200	50	400	450.00	-250.00

Demand Coefficient	100	8	*Fixed Cost*		50.00
Cost coefficients	80		10		0.6

The optimal price is \$60 and the optimal quantity is 5.

We can be more precise if we employ calculus to find the short run profit maximizing price. Let us follow the procedure explained in detail in the appendix to Chapter 2. We simply state the profit function as TR - TC. We then take the first derivative of this function, set it equal to zero and solve for Q. We can then find the optimal price by inserting this value of Q into the demand equation.

$$TR = 100Q - 8Q^2$$

$$II = 100Q - 8Q^2 - 50 - 80Q + 10Q^2 - 0.6Q^3$$

$$dII/dQ = 100 - 16Q - 80 + 20Q - 1.8Q^2 = 0$$

Using the formula for finding the roots of a quadratic equation, we arrive at:

$$Q = \frac{-4 + \text{or} - 12.65}{-3.6}$$

$$Q^* = 4.625 \qquad \text{and} \qquad P^* = \$63$$

b. In order to find the price that maximizes total revenue, we can use the spreadsheet above. We see total revenue is maximized at a price of \$52. Using calculus simply involves taking the first derivative of the total revenue function (i.e., MR), setting it equal to zero and solving for Q. Using this Q in the demand equation will give us the revenue maximizing price.

$$\ddot{A}TR/\ddot{A}Q = 100 - 16Q = 0$$
$$Q^* = 6.25$$
$$P^* = \$50$$

(Notice that the spreadsheet will also indicate a price of \$50 if the values of quantity were set for small intervals.)

c. If the firm wanted to use a linear approximation of the cubic equation, it might simply derive the linear equation in the manner shown in the figure below.

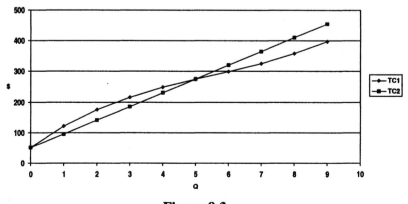

Figure 9.3

8.   If we assume that the firm uses the MR = MC rule to determine its optimal price, then it should <u>not</u> raise its price because the increase in fixed cost <u>does not</u> change marginal cost. In fact, raising price to cover the increase in fixed cost would actually move the firm <u>away</u> from its optimal price. Using a spreadsheet or calculus, we would find that given the demand and cost functions in this problem, the firm would be prompted to set its optimal price at $8.67. This is also shown in the figure below.

This figure shows that if the firm has AC_1, it would make some profit. At AC_2 (the cost that assumes a fixed cost of 30 percent more), the firm would be losing money. However, by sticking with the price, $8.67, it would at least be minimizing its losses. Furthermore, it can indeed survive (at least for the short run) if it charges this price of less than $9.00 because it at least is covering its per unit variable cost (i.e., it has a positive contribution margin).

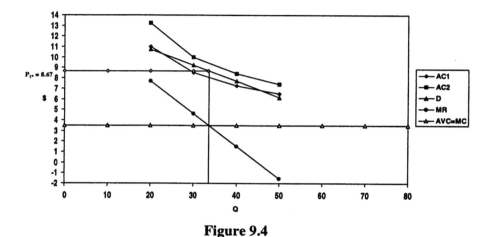

Figure 9.4

9.   Setting the derivative of the total cost function equal to the derivative of the total revenue function and solving for Q yields the same result as setting the total profit function equal to 0 and solving for Q.

$$TR = 170Q - 5Q^2$$
$$MR = 170 - 10Q$$
$$TC = 40 + 50Q + 5Q^2$$
$$MC = 50 + 10Q$$

$$MR = MC$$
$$170 - 10Q = 50 + 10Q$$
$$120 = 20Q$$
$$6 = Q^*$$

$$\pi = 170Q - 5Q^2 - 40 - 50Q - 5Q^2$$
$$= -40 + 120Q - 10Q^2$$
$$\frac{d\pi}{dQ} = 120 - 20Q = 0$$
$$120 = 20Q$$
$$6 = Q^*$$

10.   A "good" firm

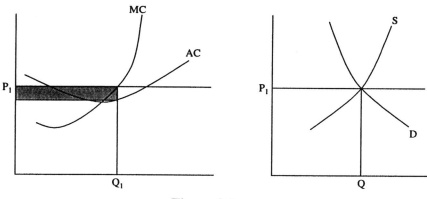

Figure 9.5

Given market price P_1, the firm is able to keep its cost structure low enough so that P = MC above AC.

A "lucky" firm

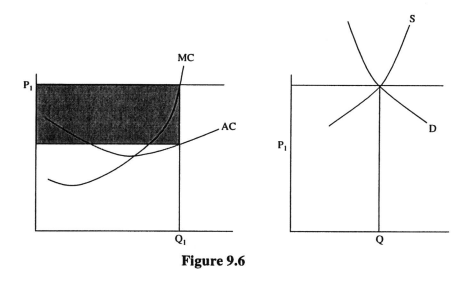

Figure 9.6

Given its cost structure, the firm is able to make an economic profit because the market price is so high.

CHAPTER 10
PRICING AND OUTPUT DECISIONS:
MONOPOLISTIC COMPETITION AND OLIGOPOLY

QUESTIONS

1. The key difference is "product differentiation."

2. a. In a pure monopoly, no one else can enter the market. Thus, the monopolist will enjoy above-normal profits as long as the demand is high relative to its cost structure.

    (Instructors may wish to discuss how realistic this is in the real world, i.e., how feasible is it for any non-regulated company to enjoy a monopoly over a long period of time.)

    b. Oligopolists may enjoy above-normal profits as long as their dominance in the market discourages companies from entering. However, as the PC market illustrates, even the giants (IBM, Apple, and Compaq) could not keep out the upstarts (AST, Leading Edge, NEC, Dell, and Northgate).

    c. Because of the ease of entry in this market, we expect any above-normal profits to eventually disappear.

    d. Because of ease of entry into the market, any above-normal profits (economic profits) will disappear.

3. Perhaps one of the most publicized examples of this is the bank credit card. In effect, the funds borrowed in the money market is the "input." Its price is the cost of these funds. The price of the "output" is the interest rate charged by the companies for the card holder's use of these funds. While money market interest rates (i.e., the cost of funds) have been falling , the interest rate charged to card holders have not. Thus, their profits on this operation have greatly increased. The reason this happens is because the money market is more "competitive" in the economic sense, while the market for credit cards is not (it is dominated by large banks such as Citibank).

4. Students should agree with this statement. A profit-maximizing firm will set a price according to the "MR=MC" rule. Firms that wish to maximize market share will try to increase their revenue. Thus, they will price their product at or near the point where MR=0. By implication, this price is lower that the one based on the MR=MC rule.

5. One of the main reasons why firms might not be able to set a price according to this rule is the difficulty and/or cost of obtaining the data on MR and MC. Indeed, firms might have to consider the trade-off between the added cost of obtaining the needed data and the added benefit of being able to maximize one's profit by following the MR=MC rule. Also, in actual business situations, volatile market conditions (demand changes, costs of certain inputs change) can change a firm's MR and MC relationships. Thus, a firm may not be able or willing to constantly adjust its price relative to the changing MR and MC.

6. Interdependence in a market means that each firm sets a price with the explicit consideration of the reactions of its competitor. Thus, in this situation, it is possible that all firms would continue to

charge the same price as everyone else for fear of either starting a price war or pricing itself out of the market.

7. A price leader provides a mechanism for everyone to begin raising prices in a more orderly and predictable fashion.

8. The usual concentration ratios could be used. Also, pricing tactics of competitors could be traced to monitor the extent of "mutual interdependence." Managers should recognize the existence of oligopoly in order to anticipate reaction by competitors to any price action that they (the managers) take.

9. a. Oligopoly in the national (or worldwide) fast food market, but monopolistic competition in local or perhaps regional markets.

    b. Oligopoly in the national (or worldwide) oil refinery market; monopolistic competition at the local retail market (i.e., neighborhood gas stations).

    c. Monopolistic competition. The top five computer manufacturers (Dell, Compaq, IBM, Hewlett-Packard, and Gateway 2000) have less than 50% of the PC market in the United States, as well as in the world market.

    d. Oligopoly (almost a duopoly if you think about Heinz and Del Monte essentially dominating the ketchup market).

    e. Oligopoly (main competitor to Procter's "Pampers" is Kimberly-Clark's "Huggies"). However, private label disposable diapers are increasing their market share.

    f. Oligopoly (there is, of course, the green box, and private store labels are also increasing in importance).

    g. Monopolistic competition. Starbucks may be alone as a national chain, but in local markets there are numerous gourmet coffee establishments.

    h. Oligopoly in national pizza chains. Monopolistic competition at the local level.

    i. Oligopoly, but because of Intel's dominance in this market, it could be called "near monopoly."

10. Advertising expenditures or perhaps R&D expenditures. An important limitation is that more than two competing firms may be involved.

11. The S-C-P paradigm says that industry structure determines industry conduct, which in turn determines industry performance. Structure is determined by the prevailing supply and demand conditions. This influences the industry's conduct—its pricing strategies, advertising, product development, etc. The industry's performance is measured in terms of how close it comes to achieving the goal of maximizing society's welfare. A concentrated industry will be less likely to arrive at this norm than an industry where competition rules.

12. (1) Threat of new entrants: relates to number of sellers in perfect and monopolistic competition.
    (2) To some extent, substitute products could also be considered a form of new competition.
    (3) Intra-market rivalry refers to the "mutual interdependence" of the oligopoly market.

(4) Buyer and supplier power have no direct relation to the characteristics of the four market types in economic theory, but are certainly important factors to consider.

PROBLEMS

1. a. Note to Instructors: We found this problem to be a good application of the concepts. We also found that this makes a good in-class assignment. If your class size allows for this, divide the class into groups of 4 to 6 students and have each be prepared to report to the class their recommendation.

    Please be aware that students may not realize at first that this problem assumes a constant MC (which therefore equals AVC). You may wish to provide this hint. However, it is interesting to let the students discover on their own about the nature of a linear total cost function.

    It is interesting to note the different approaches that students use to solve this problem. Some use the more cumbersome "TR/TC Approach," while others go right to the marginal analysis and begin comparing MR with (the constant) MC or AVC.

P_R	P_W	Q	TR	MR	E
12.50	10.00	6,000	60,000		
12.00	9.60	6,500	62,400	4.80	-1.96
11.50	9.20	7,000	64,400	4.00	-1.74
11.00	8.80	7,500	66,000	3.20	-1.55
10.50	8.40	8,000	67,200	2.40	-1.38
10.00	8.00	8,500	68,000	1.60	-1.24
9.50	7.60	9,000	68,400	0.80	-1.11
9.00	7.20	9,500	68,400	0.00	-1.00
8.50	6.80	10,000	68,000	-0.80	-0.90
8.00	6.40	10,500	67,200	-1.60	-0.80

    b. $8.75 is definitely a "sub-optimal" price as far as the students are concerned, because at that price MR < MC. In fact, this price actually falls in the inelastic portion of the demand curve. Thus, it would not even yield a maximum total revenue.

    (The elasticity of demand between $12.50 and $8.00 is -1.24, indicating that demand is elastic over this price range. However, dividing up this range into smaller intervals of $.50 reveals that $8.75 actually falls in the inelastic position of the demand curve.)

    In order to determine the profit maximizing price, we must first determine the firm's marginal cost of production. We shall assume the following costs to be variable:

Paper	$12,000
Repro Services	8,000
Binding	3,000
Shipping	2,000
Total Variable Cost	$25,000

    (Total fixed cost = $20,000)

    AVC = $4.16. Because it is constant, we can also state that it is equal to MC.

    Based on the demand schedule above, an MC of $4.16 would fall somewhere between the retail price of $12.00 and 11.50.

    c. Let us assume that the retail price is set at $12.00 (a nice round number). At this level, total cost would be $47,040 (TFC = $20,000 and TVC = $4.16 x 6500). Total profit would be $15,360.

Although this venture looks profitable, it does not seem to provide the students with economic profit. In fact, from an economic standpoint, each student would incur a loss because each student's assumed share in the profits of $3072 is not enough to cover the assumed opportunity cost of $4000. Unless the students want the experience of running their own business, the "economics" of this venture dictate that they not start this company.

d. Given the bookstore's costs (which we do not know), $8.75 may very well be its optimal price. Moreover, the store manager may want to consider the book as a "loss leader" or at least an item whose low price might attract customers into the store.

2. a. The main difference is that the inclusion or exclusion of miscellaneous cost affects the MC, thereby affecting the point at which MC = MR. When miscellaneous cost is considered to be variable, MC = $5.00. The optimal price would be about $12.75. When it is not included, MC = $4.16. Thus, the optimal price would be about $11.75.

b. In this problem, it is not likely that the law of diminishing returns would be important. However, AVC and MC could rise if for some reason factor costs rose (e.g., increase in wage rates of printers due to overtime compensation).

c. AVC and MC would probably not decrease in the short run. In the long run, they might if the students increase their operations and cut costs from economies of scale (e.g., printing and paper costs are reduced if the printer cuts the price because of higher production runs).

3. a. and b.

Firm's Demand Curve				**Industry Demand Curve**			
Price	*Quantity*	*Total Revenue*	*Marginal Revenue*	*Price*	*Quantity*	*Total Revenue*	*Marginal Revenue*
10.00	2	20		10.00	14	140	
9.00	10	90	8.75	9.00	17	153	4.33
8.00	18	144	6.75	8.00	20	160	2.33
7.00	26	182	4.75	7.00	23	161	0.33
6.00	34	204	2.75	6.00	26	156	-1.67
5.00	42	210	0.75	5.00	29	145	-3.67
4.00	50	200	-1.25	4.00	32	128	-5.67
3.00	58	174	-3.25	3.00	35	105	-7.67

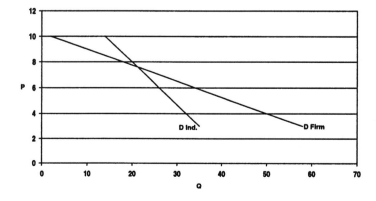

Figure 10.1

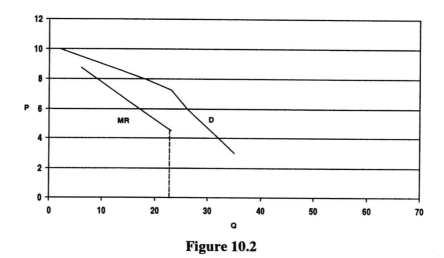

Figure 10.2

c., d., e.

The range of changes in marginal costs without impact on price is shown on above graph. It is the vertical distance between the two marginal cost curves vertically below the kink.

4. a. FALSE   Not if its loss is less than its fixed cost. See explanation of problem 1.

    b. FALSE   Even a pure monopoly has to consider the possibility of demand falling below the level sufficient to earn a profit. (For example, even if Polaroid continues to have a monopoly on cameras that use instant developing film, can they stop the erosion in demand due to the one-hour photo developing machines and cameras that record images electronically on discs?)

    c. TRUE   Other factors held constant, the entry or exit of firms will theoretically lead to this condition.

    d. TRUE   In order to maximize revenue, a firm will price its product at the point where MR=0. By implication, this must be a lower price than the point where MR=MC.

    e. FALSE   Although this is often the case, it is not always so.

    f. TRUE   Economists consider this to be true because the more opportunities for substitution that a consumer has, the more elastic the demand for a particular product tends to be. In a monopolistically competitive market, there are many more firms for consumers to choose from.

5. a. Their unit cost of goods sold might be lower because they could buy directly from the manufacturer. Also, if consumers are not brand-loyal, stores might be able to increase revenues by lowering price. Thus, private label products could be (and often are) more profitable to sell than national brands.

    b. Selling to stores could help to reduce excess capacity. If they then produce at maximum capacity, their unit costs would be minimized.

6.   a.   Regardless of their cost structure, all three would be earning less money because the demand is price inelastic over this range of prices.

b. Perhaps, depending on their respective marginal costs.

7.   a.   P = \$22 (TR = \$1980, TC = \$760)

b.   As new competitors enter the market, economic profit would decrease, eventually reaching zero.

c.   P = \$12

At this best price, the firm would be losing money. However, it would still have a positive contribution, and, therefore, it should continue to operate in the short run.

8.   a.   Firms 1 and 2 should charge \$15, Firm 3 should charge \$16.

Calculate MR:

$$40P = 1.000 - Q$$
$$P = 25 - 0.025Q$$
$$TR = 25Q - 0.025Q^2$$
$$MR = 25 - 0.05Q$$

Firms 1 and 2

$$MC = 5$$
$$MR = MC: 25 - 0.05Q = 5$$
$$400 = Q$$
$$P = 25 - 0.025 (400)$$
$$= 15$$

Firm 3

$$MC = 7$$
$$MR = MC: 25 - 0.05Q = 7$$
$$360 = Q$$
$$P = 25 - 0.025 (360)$$
$$= 16$$

b.   Firm 3's MC is higher.

c.   In the short run, probably Firm 1 because it has the highest fixed cost.

We believe that this is a very good problem for students to tackle because the answer is not as obvious as it appears. To be sure, Firm #1 has the highest "overhead" and, therefore, one would immediately assume that this would leave it most vulnerable to a price war. But this would be true as long as the price stays above about \$13. As it starts to fall below this, the higher average variable cost of Firm #3 starts to have a relatively greater impact on its profit and loss statement compared to Firm #1. For example, if the price is \$13 and assuming that both Firm #1 and Firm

#3 follow the MR = MC rule, Firm #1 loses $160 while #3 loses $120. But when the price falls to $12, #1 loses $360 while #3 loses $400.

9.   Assume that you have decided $250,000 to be the maximum amount that you could spend for the new product, leaving the rest for other products. You will probably end up spending this maximum amount (this is equivalent of a firm charging the lowest possible price).

10.   "Low-Cost Approach"

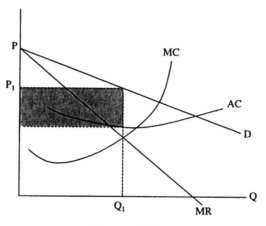

Figure 10.3

Monopolistic competitor is able to keep AC low enough so that it is able to earn an economic profit given its demand.

"Differentiation Approach"

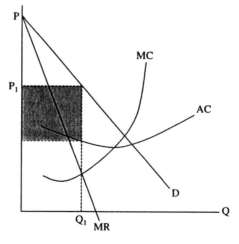

Figure 10.4

Differentiation causes D to become less elastic, thereby enabling the firm to earn an economic profit, regardless of cost structure.

CHAPTER 11
BREAK-EVEN ANALYSIS

QUESTIONS

1. Volume-cost-profit (break-even) analysis ordinarily utilizes straight-line cost curves. Thus it assumes the existence of constant average variable cost (and marginal cost), unlike the economist who usually recognizes the existence of increasing and decreasing marginal and average variable costs.

    Since V-C-P analysis also utilizes a straight line revenue curve, it does not identify a maximum profit. It shows profit increasing as a result of increases in quantity above the break-even point.

2. It analyzes short-run situations since it assumes the presence of fixed costs.

3. Fixed costs are those which are not affected by changes in quantity produced. The term constant cost usually refers to average (unit) costs remaining the same as quantity changes. (However, total cost changes as quantity changes.) In break-even analysis, average variable cost is usually considered to be constant.

4. While economists usually assume the existence of increasing and decreasing marginal costs, using constant costs over some relatively small output ranges is probably quite acceptable. Many economic cost studies have shown that average cost can be constant over intervals. And even if changing marginal (and average) costs are present, using a straight-line alternative over relatively small quantity intervals will probably not detract a great deal from the analysis.

5. Assume the following:
    $$P = 3$$
    $$AVC = 2$$
    $$TFC = 4,000$$

    Break-even quantity: $4000/(3-2) = 4000$

    a. Break-even quantity will increase.
        Assume $P = 2.80$
        Break-even quantity: $4000/(2.80-2) = 5000$

    b. Break-even quantity will decrease.
        Assume $AVC = 1.40$
        Break-even quantity: $4000/(3-1.40) = 2500$

    c. Break-even quantity will decrease.
        Assume $TFC = 3000$
        Break-even quantity: $3000/(3-2) = 3000$

6. Yes. The degree of operating leverage can be defined as a measure of business risk. A higher DOL will result in greater fluctuations in profits for any given change in quantity. A lower DOL will result in smaller profit fluctuations.

7. It probably could afford to have a plant with relatively high fixed costs. If higher fixed costs lead to a higher DOL, then a company whose production is growing in a stable manner (i.e. without significant fluctuations) will experience more rapid growth in profits than a company with a lower DOL.

8. a. Add the required profit to the total fixed costs in the numerator of the formula.

    b. Add the required unit profit to the average variable cost in the denominator of the formula.

9. No. The denominator of the DOL formula at break-even equals zero.

10. No, it is not. Corporate planning ordinarily requires detailed analysis of all component parts of the corporation.

11. V-C-P analysis can be used to make rather quick calculations showing the effect on profit of relatively small changes in quantity from those shown in the detailed plan. It is also useful in making small corrections once the plan has been established, and in arriving at some preliminary results when detailed data are not available (for instance, in the planning of new products).

PROBLEMS

1.   a. $Q = 30000/(25-10) = 30000/15 = 2000$

   b. $2000 \times 25 = 50000$

   c. | TR (3000 x 25) | 75,000 |
        |---|---|
        | TFC | 30,000 |
        | TVC (3000 x 10) | 30,000 |
        | Profit | 15,000 |

   d. $Q = 37500/(25-10) = 37500/15 = 2500$

   e. $2500 = (37500+15000)/(P-10)$
        $= 52500/(P-10)$
        $2500P - 25000 = 52500$
        $2500P = 77500$
        $P = 31$

2.   a. $5000 = 50000/(P-20)$
        $5000P - 100000 = 50000$
        $5000P = 150000$
        $P = 30$

   b. $5000 = (50000+30000)/(P-20)$
        $= 80000/(P-20)$
        $5000P - 100000 = 80000$
        $5000P = 180000$
        $P = 36$

   c. $Q = 50000/(36-30)$
        $= 50000/6$
        $= 8333$

3.   Average variable cost:

Materials	$30
Manufacturing labor (3x8)	24
Assembly labor (1x8)	8
Packing materials	3
Packing labor (6/3)	2
Shipping	10
Average variable cost	$77

   Total fixed cost $120,000

   a. $Q = 120000/(100-77) = 120000/23 = 5217$

   b. $TR = 5217 \times 100 = 521700$

c.

Quantity	2,000	4,000	6,000	8,000	10,000
TR	200,000	400,000	600,000	800,000	1,000,000
TFC	120,000	120,000	120,000	120,000	120,000
TVC	154,000	308,000	462,000	616,000	770,000
Profit	-74,000	-28,000	18,000	64,000	110,000

4.

	Last Year	Future
TR	250,000	200,000
TFC	100,000	100,000
TVC	100,000	100,000
Profit	50,000	0

No, they will no longer be profitable.

5. a. $Q = 60000/(9-6) = 60000/3 = 20000$

b. $Q = (60000+15000)/(9-6) = 75000/3 = 25000$

c. DOL at 20,000 units = undefined (denominator is zero)

DOL at 25,000 $= \dfrac{25000 \times 3}{(25000 \times 3) - 60000} = \dfrac{75000}{15000} = 5$

d. DOL at 30,000 $= \dfrac{30000 \times 3}{(30000 \times 3) - 60000} = \dfrac{90000}{30000} = 3$

6.

	Perfect Lawn	**Ideal Grass**
a.	$Q = 200000/100 = 2000$	$Q = 400000/150 = 2667$

b. $(Q \times 100) - 200000 = (Q \times 150) - 400000$
$200000 = 50Q$
$4000 = Q$

	Perfect Lawn			Ideal Grass	
TR	(4000 x 250)	1,000,000	(4000 x 250)	1,000,000
TFC		200,000		400,000
TVC	(4000 x 150)	600,000	(4000 x 100)	400,000
Profit		200,000		200,000

c. $\dfrac{4000 \times 100}{(4000 \times 100) - 200000} = \dfrac{4000 \times 150}{(4000 \times 150) - 400000} =$

$400000/200000 = 2$ $600000/200000 = 3$

d. Ideal Grass will have the higher profit, since it has higher DOL.

TR	(4500 x 250)	1,125,000	(4500 x 250)	1,125,000
TFC		200,000		400,000
TVC	(4500 x 150)	675,000	(4500 x 100)	450,000
Profit		250,000		275,000

7. a. Q = 840000/(20-8) = 70000

b. (1) Q = 1200000/(20-5) = 80000

(2) 70000 = 1200000/(P - 5)
70000P - 350000 = 1200000
70000P = 1550000
P = 22.14

c. (1) (Qx12) - 840000 = (Qx14) - 1200000
360000 = 2Q
180000 = Q

	Old		Modernized	
TR	(180000 x 20)	3,600,000	(180000 x 19)	3,420,000
TFC		840,000		1,200,000
TVC	(180000 x 8)	1,440,000	(180000 x 5)	900,000
Profit		1,320,000		1,320,000

(2)

$$\frac{180000 \times 12}{(180000 \times 12) - 840000} = \frac{180000 \times 14}{(180000 \times 14) - 1200000} =$$

$$\frac{2160000}{1320000} = 1.64 \qquad \frac{2520000}{1320000} = 1.91$$

(3) No. For the two plants to earn equal profits, sales would have to reach 180,000 units. Below this quantity, the old plant is more profitable.

8. a. 1.5 = (8000)(P - AVC)/[(8000)(P - AVC) - 10000]
(1.5) (8000)(P - AVC) - (1.5)(10000) = (8000) (P - AVC)
(12000)(P - AVC) - 15000 = (8000)(P - AVC)
(4000)(P - AVC) = 15000
(P - AVC) = 3.75

We cannot ascertain price and average variable cost, but we know that contribution (P - AVC) per unit is $3.75. Thus, profit is:

8000 x $3.75	$30,000
Less TFC	10,000
Profit	$20,000

b. Q = TFC/(P - AVC)
     = 10000/3.75
     = 2666.67

9.   a. 400000/(9 - 4) = 80000
      b. (400000 + 100000)/(9 - 4) = 100000
      c. (400000 + 100000)/(9 - 5) = 125000
      d. (450000 + 100000)/(P - 4) = 9.50
      e. (400000 + 50000)/(8 - AVC) = 3.50
      f. (400000 + 100000)/(8 - 4) = 125000

CHAPTER 12
SPECIAL PRICING PRACTICES

QUESTIONS

1. False. This statement could be true if average cost were constant and completely variable with quantity. However, if unit cost changes as more or less is produced, then what is the cost on which the mark-up should be calculated? If there are fixed costs, sales at a relatively high price (high mark-up) may not be sufficient to cover all fixed costs.

2. An example of the equity argument is given by the medical profession, when certain (low income) patients are treated at lower fees, while high income patients pay higher fees. Similarly, attorneys can charge in this manner, sometimes taking on cases at low or hardly any charge. It is quite true that in such cases people who cannot afford regular fees are benefited, while those who are able to pay more can do so with relative ease. This can be a valid argument from an equity viewpoint. However, if a firm is faced by two (or more) markets with different demand elasticities, and these markets are sealed off from one another (you cannot transfer the product or service from one market to another), charging different prices in the different markets will increase the supplier's profit. This is a case of third-degree discrimination.

3. The higher is the demand elasticity the lower will generally be the mark-up. Thus, cigarettes and orange juice probably sell at higher mark-ups.

4. Most probably, the price of coffee was the one which was raised, since presumably it has the lower elasticity of demand.

5. Both types of price leadership will occur in an oligopolistic industry. The case of barometric leadership exists when one firm (that may or may not be the largest) will change its price because of changed demand or supply conditions, and expects that others will follow. This does not always happen. In the case of dominant price leadership, a firm, usually the largest and most powerful, sets its price so that it maximizes its profits, and lets all the other firms sell as much as they wish at that price.

6. Yes. In order to maximize the total profits of the cartel, the cartel will charge a monopoly price. Output will be established at the point where the industry marginal revenue curve meets the combined marginal cost curve of the members of the cartel. Price is then charged on the demand curve. This is the same price as would be charged by a monopoly.

7. Conditions favorable to formation of cartel:

   a. Small number of large firms.
   b. Geographic proximity.
   c. Homogeneous product.
   d. High entry barriers.

8.   Yes. Monopolies can be created through regulation and licensing.

     For instance, licensing is required of various professions, such as electricians, plumbers, doctors, accountants and lawyers. The licensing boards are generally composed of members of the profession in whose interest it is to limit the number of entrants. (This statement does not mean, that there are no benefits from licensing, e.g., quality of participants. However, there is no question that the number of people in the profession will be limited.)

     In many cities, taxi cabs must have a permit (medallion) to operate. Only a limited number of these permits is available. Liquor stores must be licensed.

     In the past, several industries were regulated, e.g., the airlines. Routes and fares were specified by a government agency. Price competition did not exist.

     It might also be said that other types of government regulations (however important they may be) bring about greater concentration, and thus possibly less competition within industries. The testing of drugs as regulated by the Federal Drug Administration and requirements for pollution control set by the Environmental Protection Administration are very expensive procedures, and thus may hit small firms more than large companies. Such expenditures could create a barrier to entry into industries and thus lead to greater concentration.

9.   The Baumol model states that companies (in oligopolistic industries) have for their objective the maximization of revenue subject to a minimum profit constraint.

     The price charged by such companies would be lower than that of a profit maximizer and quantities sold will be higher. Also, changes in fixed costs could affect the quantity produced, unlike in the short-run profit maximization case.

     Revenue maximization may be important in some cases, particularly where a company tries to gain a foothold in an industry and increase its market share. This is a short-run situation. However, in the final analysis, it appears that stockholders, in the long run, are more interested in a company's profitability and cash flows. Thus the profit maximization model is under most circumstances more applicable.

10. Not necessarily. Since these prices are charged at different times of the day, they probably represent shifts in demand. Certainly, telephones are used more during the day, particularly by businesses. Telephone traffic is generally rather low at night or during weekends. However, some textbook authors include this type of pricing as an example of price discrimination.

11. If average costs are constant or nearly constant, then the methods will give same or similar answers.

12. When two passengers sitting next to one another on an airplane have paid different prices for the same trip, it would appear that this is an obvious example of price discrimination, and in some cases it certainly is. If one passenger had bought his ticket long ago (and paid for it), while the other, because of a sudden business necessity, had purchased it yesterday, it would appear that the two passengers have very different price elasticities. However, there may also be cost differences involved. An airline can do a more cost-effective job of planning its schedules when the demand is better known. Also, its cash flow from the first passenger has already occurred, and the company has had the funds for some time.

Further, there are significant swings in demand during different times in a week. Mondays, Thursdays and Fridays appear to have more (business) traffic than the other days. Thus, lower price fares may prevail during days when an airline has excess capacity.

13.   No. Within a company, mark-ups can differ from product to product. Such price difference are probably governed by differences in demand elasticity. Also, a company will change its prices and mark-ups, often in order to improve or protect its profits. This indicates that a company is moving the price along a demand curve to ascertain an optimum point.

14.   a.   Transfer pricing: a computer company which operates at different stages of production will often employ transfer pricing. Suppose the product advances through four stages: manufacture of components, assembly of components into a machine, the assembly of machines into a system, and marketing the final product. A price is established at each stage; this price becomes the unit cost for the next stage.

       b.   Psychological pricing: a price which would appeal to the public is established. For instance, a product could be priced at $19.95 instead of $20, since the small difference creates an illusion of lower price. Gasoline is usually priced at, for instance, 96.9 cents, rather than 97. Most people appear to think of this price as 96 cents.

       c.   Price skimming: the producer of a new product (with no competition) will charge a higher price. The price charged ideally would be along the demand curve (skims the demand curve) so that early customers would pay the high price they are willing to pay rather than obtain a benefit of a single price set at the equilibrium of demand and supply. As the company exhausts that part of the market willing to pay the high price, prices will be dropped, particularly as competition enters the market. Calculators, cameras and personal computers are just a few examples, where such pricing has prevailed.

       d.   Penetration pricing: a company introducing a new product will charge a relatively low price, in order to gain a foothold in the market and attain a market share over time. This may occur when a new product enters a field where other similar products are already marketed. Most frequently, penetration pricing occurs at the retail level in such items as soap, toothpaste, etc. It is also used in the restaurant business, where a new restaurant or one which wants to expand its market share will give discounts, such as two meals for the price of one.

15.   Under conditions of first- and second-degree discrimination, more may be produced than under non-discriminating monopoly. Prices will be charged along the demand curve. The demand curve thus becomes the marginal revenue curve. Thus, output could equal that which would have been produced under competitive conditions. Of course, profits accruing to the monopolist would exceed those under competitive conditions.

Under certain circumstances, production under third-degree discrimination could also be higher than under a non-discriminating monopoly. As a matter of fact, since profits are greater under conditions of discrimination, there is the possibility that a non-discriminating monopolist would find the product unprofitable and no production would take place. Thus, only under conditions of discrimination would any product be produced.

16.   A company would tend to fix its transfer prices at levels which would minimize its tax bill when shipping products among two affiliates in countries with different income tax rates.

Assume that country A has higher tax rates than B. Then, if a product were shipped from the company's facilities in A to an affiliate in B, the company would try to make its transfer prices low to decrease its profits in A and increase them in B. If components were to be shipped from B to A, then the company would charge a high transfer price to increase profits in B and decrease them in A.

Therefore, tax authorities trying to protect their tax revenues will be concerned with the level of transfer prices.

PROBLEMS

1. The total revenue function is:

    $Q = 30 - 2P$
    $P = 15 - 0.5Q$
    $TR = Q \times P = 15Q - 0.5Q^2$

    The total cost function for the two companies combined is:

    $TC = 6 + 10Q$

    The profit function for the industry is:

    $$Profit = \pi = 15Q - 0.5Q^2 - 6 - 10Q$$
    $$= -0.5Q^2 + 5Q - 6$$
    $$d\pi/dQ = -Q + 5 = 0$$
    $$Q = 5$$

    Profit is maximized at $Q = 5$
    $$\pi = -0.5 (5)^2 + 5 (5) - 6$$
    $$-12.5 + 25 - 6 = 6.5$$

    Price at this quantity: $P = 15 - 0.5 (5)$
    $$= 12.5$$

    This result can also be obtained with the following schedule:

Price	Quantity	Total Revenue	Total Cost	Profit
15.0	0			
14.0	2	28.0	26	2.0
13.0	4	52.0	46	6.0
12.5	5	62.5	56	6.5
12.0	6	72.0	66	6.0
11.0	8	88.0	86	2.0
10.0	10	100.0	106	-6.0

2. a. (1) ADULT MARKET

Price	Quantity	Total Revenue	Marginal Revenue	Marginal Cost	Total Cost	MR-MC	Profit
14.00	6	84		5.00	30.00		54.00
13.00	7	91	7.00	5.00	35.00	2.00	56.00
12.00	8	96	5.00	5.00	40.00	0.00	56.00
11.00	9	99	3.00	5.00	45.00	-2.00	54.00
10.00	10	100	1.00	5.00	50.00	-4.00	50.00
9.00	11	99	-1.00	5.00	55.00	-6.00	44.00
8.00	12	96	-3.00	5.00	60.00	-8.00	36.00
7.00	13	91	-5.00	5.00	65.00	-10.00	26.00
6.00	14	84	-7.00	5.00	70.00	-12.00	14.00
5.00	15	75	-9.00	5.00	75.00	-14.00	0.00

CHILDREN'S MARKET

Price	Quantity	Total Revenue	Marginal Revenue	Marginal Cost	Total Cost	MR-MC	Profit
13.00	4	52		5.00	20.00		32.00
12.00	6	72	10.00	5.00	30.00	5.00	42.00
11.00	8	88	8.00	5.00	40.00	3.00	48.00
10.00	10	100	6.00	5.00	50.00	1.00	50.00
9.00	12	108	4.00	5.00	60.00	-1.00	48.00
8.00	14	112	2.00	5.00	70.00	-3.00	42.00
7.00	16	112	0.00	5.00	80.00	-5.00	32.00
6.00	18	108	-2.00	5.00	90.00	-7.00	18.00
5.00	20	100	-4.00	5.00	100.00	-9.00	0.00
4.00	22	88	-6.00	5.00	110.00	-11.00	-22.00

The adult market will achieve its highest profit between prices of $12 and $13, about $56. In the children 's market, the optimum price will be $10, and the profit will be $50. Thus, the total profit, when differential prices are charged, will be about $106.

(2) COMBINED MARKET

Price	Quantity	Total Revenue	Marginal Revenue	Marginal Cost	Total Cost	MR-MC	Profit
13.00	11	143		5.00	55.00		88.00
12.00	14	168	8.33	5.00	70.00	3.33	98.00
11.00	17	187	6.33	5.00	85.00	1.33	102.00
10.00	20	200	4.33	5.00	100.00	-0.67	100.00
9.00	23	207	2.33	5.00	115.00	-2.67	92.00
8.00	26	208	0.33	5.00	130.00	-4.67	78.00
7.00	29	203	-1.67	5.00	145.00	-6.67	58.00
6.00	32	192	-3.67	5.00	160.00	-8.67	32.00
5.00	35	175	-5.67	5.00	175.00	-10.67	0.00
4.00	38	152	-7.67	5.00	190.00	-12.67	-38.00

If both adults and children are charged the same price, the a price of $11 will maximize profit at $102.

(3) This is a case of third-degree price discrimination. The elasticities of the two demand curves are different and there are no transfers between the two markets (either the admitted person is a child or it is not). Under these circumstances, by charging different prices in the two markets (i.e. exercising price discrimination), the seller can increase its profits. In this case, if different prices are charged, the maximum profit will be $106 ($56+$50), while if one price is charged, the profit will be $102.

b. First, each of the demand curves is converted, so that price is the independent variables:

$$P_A = 20 - 1Q_A$$
$$P_C = 15 - .5Q_C$$
$$P_T = 16.667 - .333Q_T$$

Marginal revenue will be calculated for each:

Adult market:
$$TR_A = 20Q_A - 1Q_A^2$$
$$MR_A = 20 - 2Q_A$$

Children's market:
$$TR_C = 15Q_C - .5Q_C^2$$
$$MR_C = 15 - 1Q_C$$

Combined market:
$$TR_T = 16.667Q_T - .333Q_T^2$$
$$MR_T = 16.667 - .667Q_T$$

Now, set marginal revenue equal to marginal cost ($5), and solve for Q and P:

Adult market:
$$20 - 2Q_A = 5 \qquad P_A = 20 - 1(7.5)$$
$$Q_A = 7.5 \qquad\qquad = 12.5$$

Children's market:
$$15 - 1Q_C = 5 \qquad P_C = 15 - .5(10)$$
$$Q_C = 10 \qquad\qquad = 10$$

Combined market:
$$16.667 - .667Q_T = 5 \qquad P_T = 16.667 - .333(17.5)$$
$$Q_T = 17.5 \qquad\qquad = 10.83$$

Total Profit:

Market with differential pricing (price discrimination)

Adult market:	7.5(12.5-5)	=	56.25
Children's market:	10(10-5)	=	50.00
Total			$106.25
Combined market:	17.5(10.83-5)	=	$102.03

As can be seen, the results are almost exactly the same as in a. The results are mathematically more precise when equations are used.

3. a.

Quantity	Price	Total Revenue	Total Cost	Total Profit	Profit Margin
0	500	0	700	-700	
1	480	480	900	-420	-87.5%
2	460	920	1100	-180	-19.6%
3	440	1320	1300	20	1.5%
4	420	1680	1500	180	10.7%
5	400	2000	1700	300	15.0%
6	380	2280	1900	380	16.7%
7	360	2520	2100	420	16.7%
8	340	2720	2300	420	15.4%
9	320	2880	2500	380	13.2%
10	300	3000	2700	300	10.0%
11	280	3080	2900	180	5.8%
12	260	3120	3100	20	0.6%
13	240	3120	3300	-180	-5.8%
14	220	3080	3500	-420	-13.6%

(1) Quantity will be between 7 and 8, and price between $340 and $360.

$$P = 500 - 20Q \qquad TC = 700 + 200Q$$
$$TR = 500Q - 20Q^2 \qquad MC = 200$$
$$MR = 500 - 40Q$$

$$MR = MC \qquad 500 - 40Q = 200$$
$$40Q = 300$$
$$Q = 7.5$$
$$P = 500 - 20(7.5)$$
$$= 500 - 150 = \$350$$

(2) Quantity will be between 12 and 13, and price will be between $240 and 260.

$$MR = 500 - 40Q = 0$$
$$Q = 12.5$$

$$P = 500 - 20(12.5) = \$250$$

(3) Quantity will be 10 and price will be $300.

$$TR = TC + 300$$
$$500Q - 20Q^2 = 700 + 200Q + 300$$
$$= 1000 + 200Q$$
$$0 = 1000 - 300Q + 20Q2$$

Solving the above quadratic equation will give Q = 10 and Q = 5. At a quantity of 5, revenue will be $2000. At a quantity of 10, revenue will be $3000. Profit will be $300 at either quantity. Revenue will be maximized at Q = 10, given the $300 minimum profit constraint.

b.

Quantity	Price	Total Revenue	Total Cost	Total Profit	Profit Margin
0	500	0	780	-780	
1	480	480	980	-500	-104.2%
2	460	920	1180	-260	-28.3%
3	440	1320	1380	-60	-4.5%
4	420	1680	1580	100	6.0%
5	400	2000	1780	220	11.0%
6	380	2280	1980	300	13.2%
7	360	2520	2180	340	13.5%
8	340	2720	2380	340	12.5%
9	320	2880	2580	300	10.4%
10	300	3000	2780	220	7.3%
11	280	3080	2980	100	3.2%
12	260	3120	3180	-60	-1.9%
13	240	3120	3380	-260	-8.3%
14	220	3080	3580	-500	-16.2%

(1) Profit will be maximized at quantity between 7 and 8, and price between $340 and $360.

(2) Revenue will be maximized at quantity between 12 and 13 and price between $240 and $260.

(3) Quantity will be 9 and price will be $320.

c. The difference between the results in a. and b. is caused by an increase in fixed costs by $80. In the usual profit maximization case in the short run, quantity and price are not affected by changes in fixed costs. In the (Baumol) revenue maximization model, however, as long as the profit constraint is not changed, a variation in fixed costs will affect price and quantity.

4. The marginal cost of paper is the sum of the marginal cost of pulp plus the marginal cost of conversion. The marginal revenue is calculated as follows:

Demand for paper	$P = 135 - 15Q$
Total revenue	$PQ = 135Q - 15Q^2$
Marginal revenue	$MR = 135 - 30Q$

All relevant numbers are shown in the following table:

Quantity	MC of Pulp	MC of Converting	MC of Paper	MR of Paper
1	18	10	28	105
2	20	15	35	75
3	25	20	45	45
4	33	25	58	15
5	43	30	73	-15

The optimum production point occurs at a quantity of 3 (tons). At that point the marginal cost of producing the pulp is just equal to the open market price. The company can thus produce the pulp in house. The price of a ton of paper when 3 tons are produced will be $90.

5. It can be assumed that the $30 purchase cost per pair is constant. In such a case the following formula can be used to arrive at price:

$$P = AC \frac{E_p}{E_p + 1} = 30 \frac{-1.8}{-0.8} = 30(2.25) = 67.50$$

Or we can arrive at the same answer by employing the mark-up formula:

$$(1 + M) = \frac{E_p}{E_p + 1} = \frac{-1.8}{-0.8} = 2.25$$

$$M = 1.25$$

Therefore, the mark-up in dollar terms is 1.25(30) = 37.50, and, therefore, the price will be $67.50.

6.   If 100 aircraft will be produced:

Fixed cost	$ 50,000,000
Variable cost (100 x $2 mill)	200,000,000
Total cost	$ 250,000,000
Markup % (10% of $400,000,000)	40,000,000

40,000,000/250,000,000 = 16%

If 150 aircraft will be produced:

Fixed cost	$ 50,000,000
Variable cost (150 x $2 mill)	300,000,000
Total cost	$ 350,000,000
Markup % (10% of $400,000,000)	40,000,000

40,000,000/350,000,000 = 11.4%

Maximum profit at the $15,000 cost level is $21,000 with a production level of 600 bushels of apples and 400 bushels of peaches. At the $25,000 cost level, the profit will be $29,000 at a production level of 900 bushels of apples and 600 bushels of peaches.

8.   The variable cost per desk for the present situation is:

Revenue (5,000 desks at $500)	$2,500,000
Contribution profit	700,000
Total variable cost	$1,800,000

Average variable cost (1,800,000/500) $360

If a price decrease of $30 increases sales to 5500 desks, the results will be:

Revenue (5500 desks at $470)	$2,585,000
Variable cost (5500 x 360)	1,980,000
Contribution profit	$ 605,000

The arc elasticity in this case is -1.54. The consultant's proposal will not maintain the contribution profit at the same level.

The price elasticity estimate of the trade publication' economist is -1.8. If the price were lowered to $470, then the total number of desk sold would be 5590. In this case

The results would be:

Revenue (5590 desks at $470)	$2,627,300
Variable cost (5590 x 360)	2,012,400
Contribution profit	$ 614,900

Even with this higher elasticity, the profit contribution would not be maintained.

9. A multinational company can charge high transfer prices when shipping products from a low tax country to a high tax country, and low transfer prices when shipping from a high tax country to a low tax country in order to minimize its combined tax bill.

    Here is an example. A company ships 1,000 units of product from its plant in country A to its assembly facility in B. The transfer price is 100 per unit. The income tax rate in A is 20% and in B 40%. A's cost of sales is 65,000 and its operating expenses are 15,000. B's cost of sales equals the revenue in A, and its operating expenses are 10,000. The finished product is sold in B at 140 per unit. The income statements are as follows:

	Country A	Country B
Revenue	100,000	140,000
Cost of sales	65,000	100,000
Gross profit	35,000	40,000
Operating expenses	15,000	10,000
Profit before taxes	20,000	30,000
Income taxes	4,000	12,000
Profit after taxes	16,000	18,000
Combined result: taxes paid	16,000	
profit after taxes	34,000	

    Now, let plant in country A charge 120 per unit. The selling price of the final product in B is, of course, still 140:

	Country A	Country B
Revenue	120,000	140,000
Cost of sales	65,000	120,000
Gross profit	55,000	20,000
Operating expenses	15,000	10,000
Profit before taxes	40,000	10,000
Income taxes	8,000	4,000
Profit after taxes	32,000	6,000
Combined result: taxes paid	12,000	
profit after taxes	38,000	

    The student should also try the opposite case, shipping from a high tax country to a low tax country.

10. The authors would favor the highest possible revenue. The highest revenue would take place at a price lower than if profits were maximized. Thus students would be on the side of the authors.

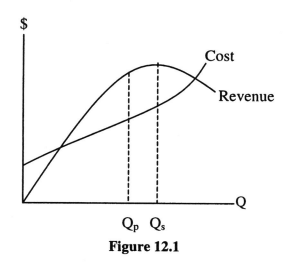

Figure 12.1

Since the demand curve has a negative slope, the unit price will be lower at Q_s (where revenue is maximized) than at Q_p (where profit is maximized).

CHAPTER 13
CAPITAL BUDGETING

QUESTIONS

1. The objective of capital budgeting is to assess the worth of projects which usually entail large expenditures of cash at the beginning of the undertaking with inflows of cash following over an extended period, usually several years.

2. a. Expansion of facilities
    b. Introduction of new or improved products
    c. Replacement of equipment
    d. Make or buy decisions
    e. Lease or buy decisions
    f. Any other decisions which entail expenditures of cash up front and cash receipts over a period of time: these could include advertising campaigns, personnel training programs and others.

3. The term "time value of money" simply says that a dollar today is worth more than a dollar tomorrow, since the dollar you receive today can earn a return (interest) over time, and therefore increase in value.

4. The net present value is calculated by summing the present value of all cash inflows and subtracting the present value of all the cash outflows. If the result is positive (i.e. the PV of inflows is larger than the present value of outflows), the project should be accepted on financial grounds. If the result is negative, the project should be rejected. If net present value equals 0, then this proposal is just earning the cost of capital, and we could be indifferent as to whether or not to accept it. However, since the proposal is just earning what is required by those who supply the funds, it could be accepted; it is a borderline decision.

5. The internal rate of return is that interest rate which equates the present value of cash inflows and outflows. If the IRR exceeds the relevant cost of capital, the project should be accepted; if the IRR is less than the cost capital, it should be rejected. If IRR equals the cost of capital, then the project is earning it required rate of return and is acceptable even though the decision here is a borderline situation.

6. True. When NPV is 0, this is because the present value of inflows and outflows is the same when discounted at the cost of capital. The IRR is the interest rate which will equate the present value of cash inflows with the present value of cash outflows—the rate that will make the net present value zero.

7. The two calculations can lead to conflicting results in the case where, for instances, two mutually exclusive projects are evaluated. While both projects could be acceptable under the NPV and IRR criteria (that is, NPV>0 and IRR>k), only one of the two projects can be accepted. In such a case the two techniques are capable of giving opposite results—one project has the higher IRR, while the other has the higher NPV. Such conflicting results can occur when the sizes of the two projects differ or the shapes of the cash inflow streams differ. The major reason for the existence of this discrepancy is that the two techniques assume different interest rates on cash inflows being returned to the project. The IRR method assumes that all cash inflows are reinvested at the IRR of the project, while the NPV method assumes reinvestment at the cost of capital. Financial economists

consider the NPV method to be the better one, because the reinvestment assumption for NPV appears to be the more logical one, and also because the NPV method is more consistent with the corporate objective of value maximization.

8. a. Initial cash outflows: this is the original investment in the project, such as the purchase of the machine, the cost of erecting a new factory, and so on.

    b. Operating cash flows: these are the periodic (annual) inflows and outflows from additional revenues, costs, cost savings, adjusted for tax effects, including those from depreciation and amortization.

    c. Changes in working capital: certain projects require, for instance, additional inventory or a higher level of accounts receivable. This represents a cash investment (just as the purchase of new equipment), and must be shown as a cash outflow at the time of the cash flow. These amounts may be returned to the projects later or at the end of the projects, and will then appear as a cash inflow.

    d. Salvage (terminal values): at the end of a project, the equipment (and/or the land and building) originally acquired may have some cash value. This must be shown (adjusted for possible tax effects) as an inflow at the end of the project.

    e. Non-cash investments: these are actually opportunity costs of using certain resources elsewhere in the business or of obtaining a cash value in the absence of their employment in the project under consideration.

9. Depreciation is not a cash expense. It is an accounting entry which is meant to consider the decrease in the value of an asset, and thus would not be considered to be a cash flow. However, as it is considered to be an expenses for income statement purposes, it will affect the tax liability of a company. Being an expense, it decreases the company's taxes, and the decrease in taxes is a decrease in the company's cash outflow—or an increase in a company's cash inflow.

10. No, it should not. The analysis of a capital budgeting project involves the consideration of an action compared to another action—or no action at all. Thus, only cash flows which are incremental to those which would exist in the absence of the new project should be considered.

11. Last year's marketing research project is considered a sunk cost, and is not relevant to the analysis. The amount has already been spent, and it will have no bearing on the current computation.

12. A company should invest in capital projects up to the point where the project with the lowest internal rate of return just equals the cost of capital of the last dollar spent. Or, it can be said that a company's optimal budget will occur at the point where the investment opportunity schedule (or curve) intersects the marginal cost of capital curve. This determination is very similar to the procedure for determining price and output of a product; a company should produce at the point where marginal cost equals marginal revenue.

13. Each component of capital (e.g. bonds, preferred stock, common stock) should be assigned a weight based on the market value of all the components combined. The cost of each component must then be determined. The weight of each component is multiplied by its respective cost; the results of these computations are added to obtain the weighted cost of capital.

14.   While there are more than two methods for determining the cost equity, the two which are probably used the most are:

   a.   The dividend growth model (the Gordon model): The first year's dividend is divided by the present price of the common stock and the expected dividend growth rate is added. In terms of an equation: $k = D_1/P_0 + g$, where k is the cost of equity capital, D_1 is the dividend in the coming year, P_0 is the current price of the stock, and g is the expected dividend growth rate.

   b.   The capital asset pricing model: add to the risk-free interest rate the product of the market risk premium and the beta (market risk) of the stock. In terms of an equation: $k = R_f + (R_m - R_f)$ beta, where R_f is the risk-free rate, and R_m is the return on a market portfolio.

15.   Beta calculates the volatility of the returns on a particular stock relative to the return on a total stock market portfolio. The greater the volatility, the greater is the riskiness of the stock. The higher risk will result in a higher required rate of return. Dominion Resources' stock fluctuates less than half as much as Compaq's stock. The higher risk of Compaq will result in a higher required rate of return.

   For example, assume that today's riskless interest rate is 5%, and the average return on a market portfolio is 12%. Then the respective rates of return, based on the Capital Asset Pricing Model, will be:

   Dominion Resources: $.05 + (.12 - .05)0.7 = .099 = 9.9\%$
   Compaq $.05 + (.12 - .05)1.55 = .159 = 15.9\%$

16.   Under the rule of capital rationing, some projects with positive net present value will not be implemented. This is because the company has limited capital expenditure to a certain sum which may not be sufficient to implement all projects which would add to the value of the company. Thus, the company is not maximizing its value.

PROBLEMS

1. This offer is too good to be true. The calculations do not consider the fact that if the buyer borrows, he/she will have to make monthly payments of $266.93. Where do these come from? If they come from his/her money market account, then the original amount, $12,000, will have to be drawn down, and thus will not earn the interest which the dealer claims will be earned. Or else, the monthly payments will have to be made from the buyer's earnings and will not be available for savings.

2. a.

		PV (at 12%)
Cash flow	year 0	$-50,000.00
	year 1	8,928.57
	year 2	15,943.88
	year 3	21,353.41
	year 4	12,710.36
	year 5	2,837.13
NPV		$ 11,773.35

    b. 21.1% (or 21%, rounded off to nearest percent)

		PV (at 21.1%)
Cash flow	year 0	$-50,000.00
	year 1	8,257.64
	year 2	13,637.72
	year 3	16,892.30
	year 4	9,299.37
	year 5	1,919.77
NPV		$ 6.80

    c. Yes, this project should be accepted. The net present value is positive and, correspondingly, the internal rate of return is higher than the cost of capital.

3. The results can be calculated in two ways.

    a. Calculate the NPV of each year's value:

Today	1	2	3	4	5	6
70.0	80.0	85.9	89.4	90.2	88.2	84.7

    The NPV in year 5 is lower than in year 4. This indicates that the collection should be sold at the end of year 4.

    b. Calculate the growth rate each year. The growth rate is actually the internal rate of return. When that becomes smaller than the cost of capital, the collection should be sold.

1	2	3	4	5	6
25.7%	18.2%	14.4%	10.9%	7.6%	5.6%

    IRR<k in year 5.

4.
Cost of new crane	$ -500,000
Cash value of old crane	70,000
Tax benefit from loss on sale of old crane (30,000 x .4)	12,000
Cash investment	$ -418,000

5.

	Year 1	Year 2	Year 3	Year 4	Year 5
Revenue	$50,000	$80,000	$80,000	$80,000	$40,000
- Cost & Exp	25,000	40,000	40,000	40,000	20,000
- Deprec.	30,000	30,000	30,000	30,000	30,000
Profit b.t	$-5,000	$10,000	$10,000	$10,000	$-10,000
Taxes	+2,000	-4,000	-4,000	-4,000	+4,000
Profit a.t	$-3,000	$6,000	$6,000	$6,000	$-6,000
+ Deprec.	30,000	30,000	30,000	30,000	30,000
Cash Flow	$27,000	$36,000	$36,000	$36,000	$24,000
PV (at 12%)	24,107	28,699	25,624	22,879	13,618

Total present value of operating cash flows: $114,927

Present value of salvage: Since book value is 0, a 40% tax must be paid on the $10,000. The remaining $6,000 must be discounted at 12% for 5 years (PV factor is .5674). Thus, present value is $3,404.

Present value of returned working capital: $15,000 x .5674 = $8,511.

Summary:
Original investment	$ -150,000
PV of operating cash flows	114,927
PV of salvage	3,404
Additional working capital	-15,000
Return of working capital	8,511
Net present value	$ -38,158

Since the net present value is negative, the purchase is not indicated.

6.
Sales	800,000
Less: Manufacturing costs (excl. depr.)	-340,000
Selling expenses (excl. depr.)	-150,000
R& D expenses	-50,000
Purchase of equipment	-30,000
Increase in working capital	-35,000
Income taxes paid	-45,000
Add: Sale of equipment	+10,000
Net cash flow in year 5	+160,000

7. If company furnishes the car, its cash flows will be as follows:

	Year 0	Year 1	Year 2	Year 3	Year 4
Original cost	$-15,000				
Current cash flow:					
Depreciation		$-3,750	$-3,750	$-3,750	$-3,750
Gasoline		-900	-900	-900	-900
Licenses & Ins.		-600	-600	-600	-600
Garaging		-300	-300	-300	-300
Maintenance		-250	-350	-450	-600
Total Expense		$-5,800	$-5,900	$-6,000	$-6150
Tax		2,320	2,360	2,400	2,460
Net Expense (a.t.)		$-3,480	$-3,540	$-3,600	$-3690
Add: Depreciation		3,750	3,750	3,750	3,750
Cash flow		$270	$210	$150	$60
Salvage (after tax)					1,500
Total cash flows	$-15,000	$270	$210	$150	$1,560
Present value	$-15,000	$245	$174	$113	$1,066
Net present value	$-13,402				

If company pays mileage:
18000 miles at $.35 per mile $6,300   Annual cost
After taxes (60%) $3,780

Present value cost (4-year annuity at 10%) $11,982

Present value cost of paying mileage is less than present value of furnishing car. Therefore, company should pay mileage.

8. If the company keeps the old machine, the cash flows will be the following:

Annual depreciation is $80,000 for six years.
    Tax shield is 40% of $80,000 or $32,000 per year.
    Present value of six-year annuity of $32,000 at 9% is $143,549.
This is the only cash flow which has to be considered for the old machine.

If the company buys the new machine:

Original cost including installation	$-1,350,000
Cash from selling old machine	400,000
Tax decrease due to loss on sale of old machine: $80,000 x .4	32,000
Savings due to lower operating costs: $250,000 per year	
Multiply by (1-tax rate) or .6: $150,000	
Present value of annuity of $150,000 for 6 years	672,888
Depreciation tax shield: $270,000 per year times tax rate (40%): $108,000	

Present value of tax shield for 5 years		420,082

Salvage:

$200,000 minus tax (40%) on profit:	$120,000	
Present value of $120,000 for 6 years		<u>71,552</u>

Present value of all cash flows		$246,522

Present value of new machine is $102,973 higher; therefore, new machine should be acquired.

9.   The dividend of $1.60 will grow by 10% to $1.76 in year 1.

$k = 1.76/40 + .1 = .144$

Thus, the cost of retained earnings is 14.4%.

$k = 1.76/38 + .1 = .146$

Thus, the cost of new equity is 14.6%.

10. $k = D_0 (1 + g)/k + g$ Remember: $D_1 = D_0(1 + g)$
$0.1 = 2(1+ g)/40 + g$
$= (2 + 2g)/40 + g$
$4 = 2 + 2g + 40g$
$2 = 42g$
$g = .0476 = 4.76\%$

11.   Market value weights:

Bonds (20,000 x $980)	$19,600,000	28%
Common stock (1,000,000 x $50)	<u>50,000,000</u>	<u>72</u>
Total	$69,600,000	100%

k of bonds: 11% x (1-tax rate)
11% x .6 = 6.6%

k of equity: 3/50 + .08 = .14 = 14%

Weighted cost of capital:

Bonds	28% x .066	.0185
Equity	72% x .14	<u>.1008</u>
Weighted cost of capital		.1193 = 11.9%

12.   a. $k_j = R_f + (k_m - R_f) \times beta$
$= .08 + (.14-.08) \times 1.3 = .08 + .078 = .158 = 15.8\%$

b.   If R_m remains at 14%, then risk premium is only 5%:
$k_j = .09 + (05) \times 1.3 = .09 + .065 = .155 = 15.5\%$

If R_m rises to 15%, the risk premium remains at 6%:
$k_j = .09 + (.06) \times 1.3 = .09 + .078 = .168 = 16.8\%$

c. $k_j = .08 + (.06) \times .8 = .08 + .048 = .128 = 12.8\%$

13. a. Calculation of net present values

Project C	Cash Flows	PV of Cash Flows
Year 0	$-40,000	$-40,000
Year 1	10,000	8,929
Year 2	10,000	7,972
Year 3	47,000	33,454
Net present value		$10,355

Project D	Cash Flows	PV of Cash Flows
Year 0	$-40,000	$-40,000
Year 1	20,500	18,304
Year 2	20,500	16,342
Year 3	20,500	14,591
Net present value		$ 9,237

Calculations of IRR

Project C	23.0%
Project D	25.0

b. Project C has the higher net present value, while project D has the higher internal rate of return. Most financial economists would agree that the net present value is the better of the two measures, and when two projects are mutually exclusive and thus only one can be accepted, the project with the higher NPV should be selected. The difference in the ranking using the two measures is really due to the difference in the interest rate used for reinvesting cash flows. In the case of the NPV calculation, cash flows are reinvested at the cost of capital, while for the IRR calculation reinvestment occurs at the project's IRR. The former assumption is usually the more reasonable one. Further, since the company's objective probably is to maximize the value of the company, maximization of the net present value of its projects is consistent with the objective.

c.

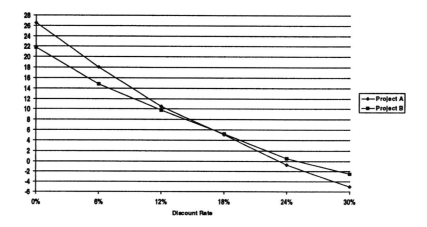

Figure 13.1

14. The projects to be undertaken are those whose combination will obtain the highest net present value while the capital expenditure remains within the limit of $340,000.

Using the trial and error method, it appears that the highest NPV can be obtained as follows:

Project	Original Investment	NPV
b. Kitchen renovation	$ 50,000	$14,000
f. Olympic size swimming pool	140,000	45,000
g. New theater arena	150,000	40,000
Total	$340,000	$99,000

CHAPTER 14
RISK AND UNCERTAINTY

QUESTIONS

1. Risk exists when there are different possible outcomes of future events but probabilities can be assigned to each of these future events. Uncertainty exists when there are different possible outcomes of future events but probabilities cannot be assigned to each of the events. "A priori" probabilities are probabilities which can be obtained by infinite repetition (e.g., a coin toss), or are based on some mathematical principle. Statistical probabilities are those where probabilities of future events are based on some past information or past experience.

2. Causes of business risk:

    a. Changes in conditions of the economy as a whole
    b. Changes in economic conditions of a specific industry
    c. Possible actions by competitors
    d. Technological changes
    e. Cost and expense changes

3. This is a discrete distribution. A discrete distribution exists when possible outcomes assume values at specific points. A continuous distribution considers all possible outcomes on a scale of values.

4. No. In a risky project, both expected value and level of risk must be considered. Risk is measured by the standard deviation. Thus, project A, which has the higher expected NPV, may have a considerably higher standard deviation. The extra NPV may not be worth the higher risk. A coefficient of variation could be calculated to ascertain the relative risk.

5. No. A standard deviation measures absolute deviations from a mean (expected value), and thus can be used to measure differences in risk for projects with the same expected value. If two projects have different expected values, then the appropriate measure is the coefficient of variation (defined as the standard deviation divided by the expected value) which measures the relative size of risk.

6. Yes. If the normal curve has a high peak and steep declines around the peak, this indicates a relatively small standard deviation—the possible outcomes will not fall far from their mean (expected value). A relatively small standard deviation signifies lower risk.

7. The table of "values of the areas under the standard normal distribution function" helps in establishing the probability of an outcome smaller or greater than a certain number. The greater is the probability of outcomes coming in below some number, the greater is the riskiness of a project.

8. The coefficient of variation—the standard deviation divided by the expected value—measures the relative risk of a set of potential outcomes.

9. Yes. Different projects may have different degrees of risk, and, therefore, different interest rates (risk adjusted discount rates) should be applied to them. The cash flows from a riskier project should be discounted at a higher discount rate.

10. The RADR method appears to be the simpler of the two techniques to apply. The certainty equivalent method requires the specification of certainty equivalent factors for each cash flow. Of

course, to be precise, the risk premium to be included in the risk adjusted discount rate should also be an exact measure. However, since all of these calculations are estimates, the risk adjusted discount rate method lends itself much more to a relatively rough calculation.

If the two measure are defined consistently, they should give the same results. This will be the case when the certainty equivalent factor $a_t = (1+r_f)^t/(1+k)^t$, where r_f is the risk-free rate, k is the risk adjusted discount rate, and ^{t} is the number of periods to be discounted.

11.   Probably. A person who buys insurance exhibits risk averse behavior while a bettor appears to exhibit risk seeking behavior.

12.   Sensitivity analysis identifies the important variables which influence results (such as the net present value of a project), and by changing each of the variables by specified amounts or percentages measures the effect of each of these changes on the final outcome. For instance, a project's cash flows are composed of cash inflows from sales and cash outflows from costs. The revenue is a function of the price of the project and the number of units sold. Each of these variables (price, quantity, and costs per unit) can be changed by some percentage from their expected values to ascertain the impact each of these (or a combination of several) changes will have on the final result.

Simulation analysis identifies the key variables and assigns probabilities to each. The results are "simulated" by the used of random numbers representing each of the probabilities. Such calculations are repeated a large number of times (each time selecting random numbers to represent probabilities) to obtain a distribution of expected values (e.g., profit, rate of return, profit margin), and the standard deviation of the distribution.

13.   Decision trees calculate and compare the expected values of specific decisions. Decision trees are particularly useful when the decision making process moves through a chronological sequence of decisions. Thus, complex decisions may be simplified through this technique. When all decisions are made at one point in time, this technique is not necessary.

14.   If a company which is analyzing a capital project has the ability to make changes while the project is in process, such "option" may improve the results. The use of real option analysis is indicated when a company can expand or contract operations, vary its inputs, abandon or postpone a project. Having such flexibility may increase the NPV compared to a project where all aspects are cast in concrete. The difference in the NPV is the value of the "real option."

PROBLEMS

1. a. $(.05)(240)+(.1)(280)+(.7)(320)+(.1)(360)+(.05)(400) = 320$

    b. $(.05)(-80)^2+(.1)(-40)^2+(.7)(0)^2+(.1)(40)^2+(.05)(80)^2 =$
         $320+160+0+160+320 = 960$
         $\sqrt{960} = 30.98$

    c. $30.98/320 = .097$

2. Expected revenue: 320

    Variance:
    $(.15)(-80)^2+(.2)(-40)^2+(.3)(0)^2+(.2)(40)^2+(.15)(80)^2 = 2560$

    Standard deviation: $\sqrt{2560} = 50.6$

    Coefficient of variation: $50.6/320 = .158$

    The expected revenues in both cases are the same. However, the standard deviation (and thus the coefficient of variation) is larger for the second set of data. When the expected values are the same, then the standard deviation measures the risk. Thus, the second situation is the more risky one. The bar graphs drawn below show that the potential outcomes in the second situation are spread more widely around the mean.

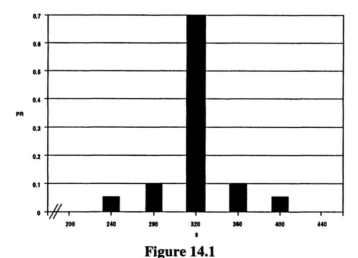

Figure 14.1

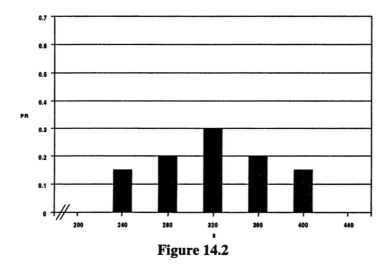

Figure 14.2

3.   *Book A*

Expected profit:	$(.2)(2000) + (.3)(2300) + (.3)(2600) + (.2)(2900)$ = 2450
Variance:	$(.2)(-450)^2 + (.3)(-150)^2 + (.2)(150)^2 + (.3)(450)^2$ = 94500
Standard deviation:	$\sqrt{94500} = 307.4$
Coefficient of variation:	307.4/2450 = .126

Book B

Expected profit:	$(.1)(1500) + (.4)(1700) + (.4)(1900) + (.1)(2100)$ = 1800
Variance:	$(.1)(-300)^2 + (.4)(-100)^2 + (.4)(100)^2 + (.1)(300)^2$ = 26000
Standard deviation:	$\sqrt{26000} = 161.2$
Coefficient of variation:	161.2/1800 = .090

The choice of Book A vs. Book B here depends on the attitude of the decision-maker toward risk. Book A has the higher profit potential but also has the higher relative risk (coefficient of variation).

4.   Investment project:

Expected return:	$(.2)(-.1) + (.6)(.1) + (.2)(.3) = .1 = 10\%$
Variance:	$(.2)(-.2)^2 + (.6)(0)^2 + (.2)(.2)^2 = .016$
Standard deviation:	$\sqrt{.016} = .1265$

U.S. Treasury bill:
Expected return: 7%   Standard deviation: 0

The investment project has a higher expected return but is considerably more risky. The decision depends on how risk averse you are.

5.   a.

   Year 1:

   Expected cash flow: $(.1)(700) + (.4)(600) + (.4)(500) + (.1)(400) = 550$

   Variance: $(.1)(150)^2 + (.4)(50)^2 + (.4)(-50)^2 + (.1)(-150)^2 = 6500$

   Standard deviation: $\sqrt{6500} = 80.6$

   Year 2:

   Expected cash flow: $(.2)(600)+(.3)(500)+(.3)(400)+(.2)(300) = 450$

   Variance: $(.2)(150)^2+(.3)(50)^2+(.3)(-50)^2+(.2)(-150)^2 = 10500$

   Standard deviation: $\sqrt{10500} = 102.5$

   Calculations of net present value and standard deviation:

   Net present value: $(550)/(1.08) + (450)/(1.08)^2 - 600 = 295.06$

   Standard deviation: $\sqrt{(6500)/(1.08)^2 + (10500)/(1.08)^4} = 115.3$

   b.

	Project A	*Project B*
Net present value	$295	$320
Standard deviation	115	125
Coefficient of variation	.3898	.3906

   Project B has a higher NPV and a higher standard deviation that Project A. However, on a relative basis, the coefficients of variation are almost the same for the two projects. While a risk averse person could be indifferent between the two projects, Project B could be preferred since it creates more net present value The creation of net present value is a legitimate objective for a corporation.

6.   Calculate the net present value of certain cash flows at the risk-free interest rate of 4%.

Year	Cash Flow	Cert Eq. Factor	Certain Cash Flow	PV at 4%
0	$-20,000	1.0	$-20,000	$-20,000
1	5,000	.9	4,500	4,327
2	5,000	.9	4,500	4,161
3	5,000	.9	4,500	4,000
4	15,000	.7	10,500	8,975

Net present value $1,463

The net present value is positive, and the project can be accepted.

7.   a.   Risk adjusted discount rate method

Year	Cash Flow	Present Value at 12%
0	$-30,000	$-30,000
1	10,000	8,929
2	10,000	7,972
3	10,000	7,118
4	20,000	12,710

Net present value $6,729

b.   Certainty equivalent method

Year	Cash Flow	Certainty Equiv. Factor		Certain Cash Flow	PV at 4%
0	$-30,000		1.0	$-30,000	$-30,000
1	10,000	$1.04/1.12$	= 0.9286	9,286	8,929
2	10,000	$1.04^2/1.12^2$	= 0.8622	8,622	7,972
3	10,000	$1.04^3/1.12^3$	= 0.8007	8,007	7,118
4	20,000	$1.04^4/1.12^4$	= 0.7435	14,869	12,710

Net present value $6,729

The resulting net present value is the same whether the risk adjusted discount rate or certainty equivalent method is used.

8.

	Project A	Project B
Net present value	500	300
Standard deviation	125	100
Coefficient of variation	.25	.33

Project A's NPV and standard deviations are higher than Project B's. Therefore, the coefficient of variation should be used to obtain the relative standard deviation. The coefficient of variation for project A is lower, and since its NPV is higher, Project A is the preferred choice.

9.   a.

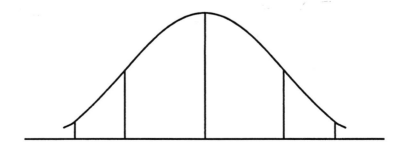

Figure 14.3

b.

$$Z = \frac{12 - 16.7}{6.2} = \frac{-4.7}{6.2} = -.76$$

Using the table for areas under the normal curve, -.76 equates to .2764. Thus, the probability of obtaining at least 12% (the required rate of return), is 77.6%.

$$Z = \frac{0 - 16.7}{6.2} = \frac{-16.7}{6.2} = -2.69$$

Again, using the table, -2.69 equates to .4964. Thus, the probability of the rate of return being at least 0 is 99.6%.

10. a.

	Year 1	Year 2	Year 3	Year 4	Year 5
Revenue	$50,000	$80,000	$80,000	$80,000	$40,000
- Cash Costs	30,000	30,000	25,000	25,000	20,000
- Deprec.	24,000	24,000	24,000	24,000	24,000
Profit b.t.	$-4,000	$26,000	$31,000	$31,000	$-4,000
Taxes	+1,360	-8,840	-10,540	-10,540	+1,360
Profit a.t.	$-2,640	$17,160	$20,460	$20,460	$-2,640
+ Deprec.	24,000	24,000	24,000	24,000	24,000
Cash flow	$21,360	$41,160	$44,460	$44,460	$21,360
P.V. @ 12%	19,071	32,813	31,646	28,255	12,120

Summary	
Original investment	$-120,000
PV of operating cash flows	123,905
PV of salvage (a.t.) 15,000 x 0.66 x 0.5674	5,617
Additional working capital	-20,000
PV or returned working capital 20,000 x 0.5674	11,348
NPV	$870

Since NPV is positive, project is acceptable.

b. (1)

	Year 1	Year 2	Year 3	Year 4	Year 5
Revenue	$55,000	$88,000	$88,000	$88,000	$44,000
- Cash Costs	28,500	28,500	23,750	23,750	19,000
- Deprec.	24,000	24,000	24,000	24,000	24,000
Profit b.t.	$2,500	$35,500	$40,250	$40,250	$1,000
Taxes	- 850	- 12,070	- 13,685	- 13,685	- 340
Profit a.t.	$1,650	$23,430	$26,565	$26,565	$660
+ Deprec.	24,000	24,000	24,000	24,000	24,000
Cash flow	$25,650	$47,430	$50,565	$50,565	$24,660
PV at 12%	22,902	37,811	35,991	32,135	13,993

Summary

Original investment	$-120,000
PV of operating cash flows	142,832
PV of salvage (a.t.) 30,000 x 0.5674	11,235
Additional working capital	- 20,000
PV or returned working capital 20,000 x 0.5674	11,348
NPV	$25,415

The best case presents a high positive NPV.

b. (2)

	Year 1	Year 2	Year 3	Year 4	Year 5
Revenue	$45,000	$72,000	$72,000	$72,000	$36,000
- Cash Costs	31,500	31,500	26,250	26,250	21,000
- Deprec.	24,000	24,000	24,000	24,000	24,000
Profit b.t.	$-10,000	$16,500	$21,750	$21,750	$-9,000
Taxes	+3,400	-5,610	-7,395	-7,395	+3,060
Profit a.t.	$-6,600	$10,890	$14,355	$14,355	$-5,940
+ Deprec.	24,000	24,000	24,000	24,000	24,000
Cash flow	$17,400	$34,890	$38,355	$38,355	$18,060
P.V. @ 12%	15,536	27,814	27,300	24,375	10,248

Summary

Original investment	$-120,000
PV of operating cash flows	105,273
PV of salvage (a.t.)	0
Additional working capital	-20,000
PV or returned working capital 20,000 x 0.5674	11,348
NPV	$-23,379

The worst case result is highly negative.

11.

Prob. Year 1	PV CF Year 1	Prob. Year 2	PV CF Year 2	Total PV CF	Joint Prob.	PV CF x Prob.
Large						
		0.3	180	280	0.09	25.20
0.3	100	0.5	90	190	0.15	28.50
		0.2	60	160	0.06	9.60
		0.3	80	120	0.15	18.00
0.5	40	0.5	40	80	0.25	20.00
		0.2	20	60	0.10	6.00
		0.3	50	30	0.06	1.80
0.2	-20	0.5	30	10	0.10	1.00
		0.2	-30	-50	0.04	-2.00
TOTAL						108.10

Prob. Year 1	PV CF Year 1	Prob. Year 2	PV CF Year 2	Total PV CF	Joint Prob.	PV CF x Prob.
Small						
		0.3	100	160	0.09	14.40
0.3	60	0.5	60	120	0.15	18.00
		0.2	40	100	0.06	6.00
		0.3	70	110	0.15	16.50
0.5	40	0.5	40	80	0.25	20.00
		0.2	30	70	0.10	7.00
		0.3	50	70	0.06	4.20
0.2	20	0.5	30	50	0.10	5.00
		0.2	10	30	0.04	1.20
TOTAL						92.30

	Large	Small
Net Present Value	$58,100	$52,300
Standard Deviation	81,270	32,090
Coeff. of Variation	1.4	0.6

While the NPV of purchasing the large press is higher, so is its standard deviation and coefficient of variation. An outcome one standard deviation below the expected value would incur a negative NPV ($23,170) if the large press were bought, but a positive NPV ($20,210), if the small press were purchased. A risk-averse business person would most likely opt for the small press.

12.   The NPV of the "research" alternative is $328,000, while the NPV of the "no research" alternative is $345,000. Thus it appears that purchasing the patent without additional research is the better alternative. However, we must remember that we have not considered risk in this calculation. Chances are that the "no research" alternative is riskier.

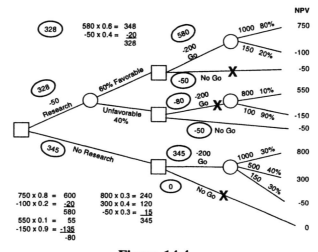

Figure 14.4

13.   a.   Result for the first five years:

PV of $55,000/year at 12%	$198,263
Original investment	250,000
NPV	$-51,737

The result of the first five years is negative—not acceptable.

b.   Second five years:

Expected annual cash inflow	
$55,000 with a 50% probability	$27,500
$100,000 with a 50% probability	50,000
Expected annual cash inflow	$77,500
PV of $77,500/year at t = 5	$279,370
Investment at t = 5	150,000
NPV at t = 5	$129,370
NPV at t = 0	$73,408
Less: NPV of first five years	-51,737
Total NPV	$21,671

The project is now acceptable, and the value of the option is $73,408.

CHAPTER 15
GOVERNMENT AND INDUSTRY

QUESTIONS

1.   * Provides a legal and social framework within which market participants operate.
       * Maintains competition (protects against anti-competitive behavior).
       * Redistributes income.
       * Reallocates resources that are not efficiently allocated because of market externalities.
       * Stabilizes the aggregate economy (strives to maintain full employment and stable prices).

2.   Market externalities are either benefits that are not accrued (i.e., benefit externalities) or costs (i.e., cost externalities) that are not incurred by either the buyers or sellers in a given market.

     Benefit Externalities: When this type of externality occurs, buyers tend to understate their true demand for a product. Consequently the product's price is lower than it should be, leading to an underallocation of society's resources (because of a lower quantity supplied) in this market.

     Cost Externalities: When this type of externality occurs, sellers tend to overstate their true supply for this product. Consequently, the product's price is lower than it should be, leading to an overallocation of society's resources (because of a greater quantity demanded) in this market.

3.   The government attempts to "internalize" benefit externalities by taxing the public and then spending the tax revenue in a manner that it believes is commensurate with the true demand for a particular social good.

     The government attempts to "internalize" the externalities by imposing fines or taxes on companies that operate in those industries in which these externalities exist. This presumably raises their costs closer to the true costs.

4.   Let us suppose that this chemical company was dumping its industrial waste into a river. The spokesperson could say that the use of this river represents an economic cost that the company (and its customers) should be paying for but are not. In other words, the use of this river is a cost externality. By fining this company, the government is simply forcing the company to sell the chemicals at a market price that is closer to what it should be, given all of the costs of production (including the cost externalities).

5.   We believe that students and instructors should basically agree with this statement, although some may prefer to use "self-interest" instead of "selfish." Behind both the supply and demand in a market economy lies the motivating factor of self-interest. Producers seek to maximize their profits given their cost and the market demand and price. Consumers wish to maximize their benefits from the use of a particular good or service, given the market supply and price. If producers are able to avoid paying for certain costs, then they will certainly do so in order to earn additional profit. If consumers are able to accrue certain benefits from a good without having to pay for them, then they will certainly not demand this product to the extent that they really believe it is worth to them.

6.   The Coase theorem states that, in the presence of cost externalities, government intervention may not be necessary if property rights are clearly defined. In such a case, bargaining between the two

parties will, under many circumstances, arrive at an optimal solution. This result will be achieved at the same level that would have been achieved by a correct taxation policy.

7. We, the authors, do not think so. There is enough potential competition from the likes of Sun and Java, and the new "free" Unix-based software called "Linux." Moreover, with technology changing so rapidly, the current operating systems on the current type of PC may go the way of the buggy whip (e.g., wireless personal digital assistants, smart cards, PC on a chip, etc.).

8. According to industry reports, American Express was awarded contracts with only certain government agencies. It is our guess that they probably needed the volume of ALL the federal government's business to earn at least a normal profit on this type of business. Since they apparently could not, they decided to exit the business of providing travel and entertainment cards for the federal government.

9. Mergers are usually done for purposes of cost cutting (e.g., does the newly formed company need two information systems departments?). All of the industries listed in the question have companies that merged for cost-cutting reasons. But in some cases, mergers are done to increase revenue as well. For example, Bell Atlantic merged with Nynex so that they could provide service from "Maine to Virginia." Part of this may be marketing "hype." However, a real reason for merging in order to gain revenue is the need among wireless telephone services to provide national (and even international) coverage. As this manual is being prepared, Bell Atlantic is considering an alliance with Vodaphone's AirTouch in order to try to match the national coverage now being offered by AT&T. Ostensibly, the newly combined DaimlerChrysler is now able to offer consumers a complete line of cars, trucks, sports utility vehicles and vans from the very low end to the top of the line. The ability to offer such a full line of cars might very well enable the company to increase its revenue as well as decrease its cost.

TEST BANK

CHAPTER 1—INTRODUCTION

1. Which of the following is an example of how the question of "what goods and services to produce?" is answered by the command process?

    *   a. government subsidies for affordable housing
        b. laws regarding equal opportunity in employment
        c. government allowance for the deduction of interest payments on private mortgages
        d. government regulations concerning the dumping of industrial waste

2. Opportunity cost is best defined as

        a. the amount given up when choosing one activity over all other alternatives.
    *   b. the amount given up when choosing one activity over the next best alternative.
        c. the opportunity to earn a profit that is greater than the one currently being made.
        d. the amount that is given up when choosing an activity that is not as good as the next best alternative.

3. In a market economy, which of the following is the most important factor affecting scarcity?

    *   a. the needs and wants of consumers
        b. the price of the product
        c. the degree to which the government is involved in the allocation of resources.
        d. all of the above are equally important.

4. Which of the following is not considered by economists to be a basic resource or factor of production?

    *   a. money
        b. machinery and equipment
        c. technology
        d. unskilled labor

5. Select the group that best represents the basic factors of production.

    *   a. land, labor, capital, entrepreneurship
        b. land, labor, money, management skills
        c. land, natural resources, labor, capital
        d. land, labor, capital, technology

6. Which of the statements below best illustrates the use of the market process in determining the allocation of scarce resources?

        a. "Let's make this product because this is what we know how to do best."
    *   b. "Although we're currently making a profit on the products we make, we should consider shifting to products where we can earn even more money."

    c. "Everyone is opening video stores, why don't we?"
    d. "We can't stop making this product. This product gave our company its start."

7.   Which of the following is the best example of "what goods and services should be produced?"

    a. the use of a capital intensive versus a labor intensive process of manufacturing textiles
*   b. the production of army helicopters versus the production of new commercial jet aircraft
    c. the manufacturing of computer workstations in Hong Kong or in Germany
    d. the leasing versus the purchasing of new capital equipment

8.   Which of the following is the best example of "how should goods and services be produced?

    a. adherence to technical specifications in the production of jet aircraft.
    b. the production of jet aircraft for the air force or for a commercial airline.
*   c. the use of additional full-time workers versus the use of supplementary part-time workers
    d. the production of a new manufacturing facility

9.   Which of the following is the best example of opportunity cost?

    a. a company's expenditures on a training program for its employees.
    b. the rate of return on a company's investment
    c. the amount of money that a company can earn by depositing excess funds in a money market fund
*   d. the amount of profit that a company forgoes when it decides to drop a particular product line in favor of another one

10.   From the standpoint of a soft drink company the question of "What goods and services should be produced" is best represented by which of the following decisions:

    a. whether or not to hire additional workers
    b. whether or not to increase its advertising
    c. whether or not to shut down selected manufacturing facilities
    d. all of the above are examples
*   e. none of the above are examples

11.   Scarcity is a condition that exists when

    a. there is a fixed supply of resources.
    b. there is a large demand for a product.
*   c. resources are not able to meet the entire demand for a product.
    d. all of the above.

12.   Managerial economics is best defined as

    a. the study of economics by managers.
    b. the study of the aggregate economic activity.
*   c. the study of how managers make decisions about the use of scarce resources.
    d. all of the above are good definitions.

13. In the text, the authors refer to "Stage II" of the process of changing economics as:

    a. demand management
*   b. cost management
    c. diminishing returns
    d. profit taking

14. Which of the following is the best example of the "command" process?

    a. MCI-Worldcom buys Sprint.
    b. Striking auto workers force General Motors to shut down its factories.
    c. Banks raise their fees on late payments by credit card holders.
*   d. The FCC requires local telephone companies to provide access to their local networks before being able to offer long distance service.

15. A critical element of entrepreneurship (as opposed to managerial skills) is

    a. leadership skills.
*   b. risk taking.
    c. technology.
    d. political skills.

16. In the text, a key factor in the changing "economics of a business" is:

    a. the need to grow revenues
*   b. increasing competition
    c. rising labor costs
    d. the need to expand market share

CHAPTER 2—THE FIRM AND ITS GOALS

1.   Transaction costs include:

    a.   costs of negotiating contracts with other firms.
    b.   cost of enforcing contracts.
    c.   the existence of asset-specificity.
*   d.   all of the above.

2.   A company will strive to minimize

    a.   transaction costs.
    b.   costs of internal operations.
*   c.   total costs of transactions and internal operations combined.
    d.   variable costs.

3.   Company goals that are concerned with creating employee and customer satisfaction and maintaining a high degree of social responsibility are called _____objectives.

    a.   social
*   b.   noneconomic
    c.   welfare
    d.   public relations

4.   _____ risk involves variation in returns due to the ups and downs of the economy, the industry and the firm.

    a.   structural
    b.   fluctuational
*   c.   business
    d.   financial

5.   _____ risk concerns the variation in returns that is induced by leverage.

    a.   business risk
    b.   premium
    c.   business
*   d.   financial

6.   Unlike an accountant, an economist measures costs on a(n) _____ basis.

    a.   implicit
*   b.   replacement
    c.   historical
    d.   conservative

7.   When a company manages its business in such a way that its cash flows over time, discounted at the appropriate discount rate, will cause the value of the company's common stock to be at a maximum, it is called _____ maximization.

     a.   profit
*   b.   stockholder wealth
     c.   asset
     d.   none of the above

8.   When a firm earns a normal profit, its revenue is just enough to cover both its _____ cost and its _____ cost.

*   a.   accounting; opportunity
     b.   accounting; replacement
     c.   historical; replacement
     d.   explicit; accounting

9.   A large corporation's profit objective may not be profit or wealth maximization, because

     a.   stockholders have little power in corporate decision making.
     b.   management is more interested in maximizing its own income.
     c.   managers are overly concerned with their own survival and may not take all prudent risks.
*   d.   all of the above.

10.   Accounting costs

*   a.   are historical costs.
     b.   are replacements costs.
     c.   usually include implicit costs.
     d.   usually include normal profits.

11.   The calculation of stockholder wealth involves

     a.   the time-value of money concept.
     b.   the cash flow stream.
     c.   business and financial risk.
*   d.   all of the above.

12.   As an objective, the maximization of profits ignores

     a.   the timing of cash flows
     b.   the time-value of money concept.
     c.   the riskiness of cash flows.
*   d.   all of the above.

13.   Another name for stockholder wealth maximization is

     a.   profit maximization.
     b.   maximization of earnings per share.
*   c.   maximization of the value of the common stock.
     d.   maximization of cash flows.

14.   MVA (Market Value Added)

    a.   will always be a positive number.
*   b.   may be a negative number.
    c.   measures the market value of the firm.
    d.   none of the above.

CHAPTER 3—SUPPLY AND DEMAND

1.   How long is the "short-run" time period in the economic analysis of the market?

    a.   three months or one business quarter
*   b.   total time in which sellers already in the market respond to changes in demand and equilibrium price.
    c.   total amount of time it takes new sellers to enter the market
    d.   total amount of time it takes original sellers to leave the market

2.   A new taco-making machine that is similar in size and cost to hot dog carts has encouraged more street vendors to begin selling tacos. What <u>short-run</u> impact do you think this might have on the market for hot dogs?

*   a.   decrease in the demand for hot dogs
    b.   increase in the demand for hot dogs
    c.   decrease in the supply of hot dogs
    d.   increase in the supply of hot dogs

3.   Which of the following is <u>not</u> a non-price determinant of demand?

    a.   tastes and preferences
    b.   income
*   c.   technology
    d.   future expectations

4.   Which of the following is <u>not</u> a nonprice determinant of supply?

    a.   costs
    b.   technology
*   c.   income
    d.   future expectations

5.   Which of the following statements is <u>not</u> true?

    a.   an increase in demand causes equilibrium price and quantity to rise.
    b.   a decrease in demand causes equilibrium price and quantity to fall.
    c.   an increase in supply causes equilibrium price to fall and quantity to rise.
*   d.   a decrease in supply causes equilibrium price to rise and quantity to rise.

6.   A short-run time period is

    a.   the period of time in which sellers already in the market respond to a change in equilibrium price by adjusting the amount of their fixed inputs
*   b.   the amount of time it takes for the market price to reach a new equilibrium as a result of some initial change in supply or demand.
    c.   the amount of time it takes for sellers and buyers to decide on whether to enter a new market.
    d.   the amount of time it takes for buyers to change their purchasing habits as a result of a change in market price.

7.   Which of the following would cause a decrease in the demand for fish?

    a.   the price of red meat increases.
    b.   the price of fish increases.
*   c.   the price of chicken decreases.
    d.   the number of fishing boats decreases.

8.   Which of the following would cause a short run decrease in the quantity supplied of personal computers?

*   a.   the price of workstations decreases.
    b.   the price of PC software decreases.
    c.   the number of PC manufacturers decreases.
    d.   the cost of manufacturing PCs decreases.

9.   Which of the following will not cause a short run shift in the supply curve?

    a.   a change in the number of sellers
    b.   a change in the cost of resources
*   c.   a change in the price of the product
    d.   a change in future expectations.

10.   In the short run, a change in the equilibrium price will

    a.   always lead to inflation.
    b.   cause a shift in the demand curve.
    c.   cause a shift in the supply curve.
*   d.   cause a change in the quantity demanded or supplied.

11.   Which of the following applies most generally to supply in the long run?

    a.   Average cost must decline.
*   b.   Sellers are able to make adjustments in all of their factors of production.
    c.   Sellers are only able to make adjustments in their variable factors of production.
    d.   All original sellers will leave the market.

12.   A movement along the demand curve may be caused by

    a.   a change in non-price determinants of demand.
    b.   a change in consumer expectations.
    c.   a change in demand.
*   d.   a change in supply.

13.   The rationing function of price

    a.   occurs when there is a movement of resources into or out of markets as a result of changes in the equilibrium market price.
    b.   is also known as the guiding function of price.
*   c.   occurs when consumers change their tastes and preferences.
    d.   occurs only when the market experiences severe shortages.

14. The switch to the use of HFCS from sugar in soft drinks was prompted in large part by its relatively lower price. Assuming a competitive market, what effect would this change have on the equilibrium price and output for soft drinks?

    a. price rises, output falls
*   b. price falls, output rises
    c. price rises, output rises
    d. price falls, output falls

15. Which of the following best describes the "guiding function" of price?

a. In response to the surplus or shortage in two markets, price serves as a"guiding function" by decreasing in one market and increasing in the other market in the short run.
*   b. The guiding function of price is the movement of resources into or out of markets in response to a change in the equilibrium price of a good or service.
    c. The guiding function of price occurs when the market price changes to eliminate the imbalance between supply and demand caused by a shortage or surplus at the original price.
    d. The guiding function usually occurs in the short run while the rationing function usually occurs in the long run.

16. Which of the following best applies to the distinction between the "long run" and the "short run"?

    a. The short run is a period of approximately 1-6 months while the long run is any time frame longer.
    b. In the short run, only new firms may enter, while in the long run firms may either enter or exit the market
*   c. The rationing function of price is a short run phenomenon whereas the guiding function is a long run phenomenon.
    d. All of the above statements are correct.

17. Which of the following would indicate that price is temporarily below its market equilibrium?

    a. There are a number of producers who are left with unwanted inventories.
*   b. There are a number of customers who must be placed on waiting lists for the product.
    c. Firms decide to leave the market.
    d. The government must step in and subsidize the product.

18. Comparative statics analysis in economics is best illustrated as

*   a. the comparison of equilibrium points before and after changes in the market have occurred.
    b. a comparison of two types of markets.
    c. the comparison of the percentage of change in the one variable divided by the percentage change in the other variable.
    d. an analytical technique used to show best case scenarios of demand and supply curves.

19. The guiding function of price is

    a. the movement of price to clear the market of any shortages or surpluses.
    b. the use of price as a signal to guide government on the use of market subsidies.
*   c. a long run function resulting in the movement of resources into or out of markets.
    d. the movement of price as a result of changes in the demand for a product.

20.   If the price of a substitute product increases, which of the following is most likely to happen in the market for the product under consideration in the short run?

      a.   supply will increase.
      b.   firms will leave the market.
*   c.   firms in the market will devote more of their variable inputs to the making of this product.
      d.   firms in the market will devote less of their variable inputs to the making of this product.

21.   Which of the following would lead to a short-run market surplus for fish?

      a   the price of fish increases.
*   b.   a new government study shows that fish have a greater risk of contamination from pollution.
      c.   an increase in the price of chicken.
      d.   a decrease in the number of fishing companies.

22.   Suppose demand is expressed as $Q_D = 300 - 50P$. If we want to make this equation consistent with the typical supply and demand diagram, this equation must be stated as:

      a. $P = 300 - 50Q$
*   b. $P = 6 - .02Q$
      c. $P = 50 - 300Q$
      d. $Q = 6 - .02P$

23.   Which of the following refers to a shift in the demand curve?

*   a.   "This new advertising campaign should really increase our demand."
      b.   "Let's drop our price to increase our demand."
      c.   "We dare not raise our price because our demand will drop."
      d.   "If new sellers enter the market, the demand for the product is bound to increase."

24.   In a perfectly competitive market, if the cost of production falls, we can expect:

      a.   sellers to earn more profit.
      b.   sellers to earn less because price will fall.
*   c.   consumers to buy more.
      d.   consumers to buy less.

25.   Which of the following gives the <u>clearest</u> indication of a <u>perfectly</u> competitive market?

      a.   the product is standardized
      b.   there is relatively easy entry into the market
*   c.   buyers and sellers are price takers
      d.   the buyers and sellers are relatively small
      e.   all of the above are equally clear indicators

26.   In 1998, the following event(s) caused a significant decline in the price of sugar:

      a.   favorable weather in important sugar growing countries
      b.   economic conditions in Asia reduced sugar demand
      c.   lowered demand for other products made of sugar
*   d.   all of the above.

27. Which of the following will result in an increase in demand for residential housing in the short run?

    a. a decrease in the price of lumber
    b. an increase in the wages of carpenters
   *   c. an increase in real household incomes
    d. a decrease in the prices of residential housing

28. A decrease in the price of personal computers can result from

    a. a decrease in the price of chips.
    b. improvements in methods of assembling computers.
    c. an increase in the gross national product.
   *   d. both a. and b.

29. Which of the following can result in an increase in the supply of residential housing in the short run?

   *   a. a decrease in the price of lumber
    b. a decrease in real household incomes
    c. an increase in the wages of electricians
    d. none of the above

30. Which of the following is a key determinant of both supply and demand?

    a. income
   *   b. future expectations
    c. tastes and preferences
    d. sales tax

31. Which of the following could cause a long-run shift in demand as part of the "guiding function of price"?

    a. a change in tastes and preferences
   *   b. an increase in price caused by a shift in supply
    c. income shift caused by an economic recession
    d. an increase in number of buyers

32. A market is in equilibrium when

    a. supply is equal to demand.
    b. the price is adjusting upward.
   *   c. the quantity supplied is equal to the quantity demanded.
    d. tastes and preference remain constant.

33. Which of the following indicates that there is a shortage in the market?

    a. demand is rising
    b. demand is falling
   *   c. price is rising
    d. price is falling

34.   The rationing function of price occurs when

*   a.   price is falling, thereby reducing a market surplus.
       b.   new sellers enter the market.
       c.   buyers leave the market.
       d.   none of the above.

CHAPTER 4 AND APPENDIX A—DEMAND ELASTICITY

1. The sensitivity of the change in quantity demanded to a change in price is called

    a. income elasticity.
    b. cross-elasticity.
 * c. price elasticity of demand.
    d. coefficient of elasticity.

2. The sensitivity of the change in quantity consumed of one product to a change in the price of a related product is called

 * a. cross-elasticity.
    b. substitute elasticity.
    c. complementary elasticity.
    d. price elasticity of demand.

3. The minimum wage is an example of a government imposed

    a. price control.
    b. price ceiling.
    c. price floor.
    d. both a) and b).
 * e. both a) and c).

4. A product that is similar to another, and can be consumed in place of it, is called

    a. a normal good.
    b. an inferior good.
    c. a complementary good.
 * d. a substitute good.

5. Two goods are _____ if the quantity consumed of one increases when the price of the other decreases.

    a. normal
    b. superior
 * c. complementary
    d. substitute

6. A tax that is imposed as a specific amount per unit of a product is a(n)

 * a. excise or specific tax.
    b. sales or ad valorem tax.
    c. compound duty.
    d. income tax.

7.   The government unit that wants to achieve "revenue enhancement" will find it considerably more favorable to enact an excise tax on products whose demand is

    a. highly elastic.
    b. relatively elastic.
*   c. highly inelastic.
    d. unitary elastic.

8.   A product consumed in conjunction with another is called a(n)

    a. inferior good.
*   b. complementary good.
    c. normal good.
    d. substitute good.

9.   Two products are _____ if the quantity consumed of one increases when the price of the other increases.

    a. normal
    b. inferior
    c. complementary
*   d. substitutes

10.   When total revenue increases from $18,000 to $26,000 when quantity increases from eight to ten, marginal revenue is equal to

    a. $3,000.
*   b. $4,000.
    c. $8,000.
    d. $2,600.

11.   When total revenue reaches its peak (elasticity equals 1), marginal revenue reaches

    a. 1.
*   b. zero.
    c. -1.
    d. cannot be determined from the information provided.

12.   The demand for items that go into the production of a final product is called

    a. marginal demand.
    b. aggregate demand.
    c. partial demand.
*   d. derived demand.

13. Remembering that demand elasticity is defined as the percentage change in quantity divided by the percentage change in price, if price decreases and, in percentage terms, quantity rises more than price has dropped, total revenue will

*   a. increase.
       b. decrease.
       c. remain the same.
       d. either increase or decrease.

14. When a one percent change in price results in a one percent change in quantity demanded in the opposite direction, demand is

       a. relatively inelastic.
*   b. unitary elastic.
       c. perfectly elastic.
       d. perfectly inelastic.

15. The owner of a produce store found that when the price of a head of lettuce was raised from 50 cents to $1, the quantity sold per hour fell from 18 to 8. The arc elasticity of demand for lettuce is

       a. -0.56.
*   b. -1.15.
       c. -0.8.
       d. -1.57.

16. When purchases of tennis socks decline following an increase in the price of tennis sneakers (other things remaining equal), the relationship between these two items can be described as

       a. substitutable.
*   b. complementary.
       c. unique.
       d. ordinary.

17. If the income elasticity coefficient equals 1, the proportion of a consumer's income spent on a given product after a change in income will be _____ the proportion of income spent on that product prior to the income change.

       a. greater than
       b. less than
*   c. equal to
       d. either greater than or equal to

18. In general, if there are many good substitutes for a given product, the demand elasticity will be

*   a. high.
       b. low.
       c. indeterminate.
       d. zero.

19.   The derived demand curve for a product component will be more inelastic

    a.   the larger is the fraction of total cost going to this component.
*   b.   the more inelastic is the demand curve for the final product.
    c.   the more elastic are the supply curves of cooperating factors.
    d.   the less essential is the component in question.

20.   As income rise and consumers feel "better off," they will shift consumption away from _____ goods toward goods more commensurate with their improved economic status.

*   a.   inferior
    b.   superior
    c.   normal
    d.   inelastic

21.   If the consumption of sugar does not change at all following a price increase from 49 cents per pound to 58 cents per pound, the demand for sugar is considered to be

    a.   relatively inelastic.
    b.   perfectly elastic.
*   c.   perfectly inelastic.
    d.   unitary elastic.

22.   When the consumption of chicken (whose price has not changed) increases following an increase in the price of beef, the two products can be considered to be

    a.   complements.
*   b.   substitutes.
    c.   unrelated.
    d.   correlated.

23.   Because there is less opportunity for substitution the broader the definition of a product (e.g., bread in general), rather than a particular brand or variety of bread, the (higher; *lower) its price elasticity will tend to be.

24.   When a one percent change in price causes a change in quantity demanded greater than one percent, demand for the product is

*   a.   relatively elastic.
    b.   relatively inelastic.
    c.   perfectly elastic.
    d.   unitary elastic.

25.   If the income elasticity of a particular product is -0.2, it would be considered

    a.   a superior good.
    b.   a normal good.
*   c.   an inferior good.
    d.   an elastic good.

26.   If a firm decreases the price of a product and total revenue decreases, then

    a.   the demand for this product is price elastic.
*   b.   the demand for this product is price inelastic.
    c.   the cross elasticity is negative.
    d.   the income elasticity is less than 1.

27.   The following form of a demand curve will exhibit constant elasticity over its relevant range:

    a. $Q = a - bP$
    b. $Q = a/P^b$
*   c. $Q = a^{P-b}$
    d.   none of the above.

28.   A product has an arc demand elasticity of -3. At a price of $6, 1,000 units are sold per period. If price is lowered to $5.647, the quantity sold per period will be _____ units.

Answer: 1,200

29.   A product has an arc elasticity of -2.3. At a price of $8, 500 units are sold per period. In order to sell 600 units per period, the price will have to be decreased to _____.

Answer: $7.392

30.   A product has an arc price elasticity of -0.8. At a price of $7, 1,000 units are sold per period. In order to sell 1,200 units, price will have to be lowered to _____, and the revenue will be _____.

Answers: $5.571, $6,685

31.   The arc price elasticity of a product is -0.75. At a price of $4, 700 units are sold per period. If price is raised to $4.50, the units sold per period will be _____, and the revenue will become _____.

Answers: 641, $2,884

32.   A product's demand function if of the form q = 18 - p. At a quantity of 5, the point elasticity is _____. Between quantities of 6 and 7, the arc elasticity is _____.

Answers: -2.6, -1.77

33.   A product's demand function is of the form q = 20 - 0.75p. At a price of $14, the point elasticity will be _____. Between prices of $11 and 12, the arc elasticity will be _____.

Answers: -1.11, -0.76

CHAPTER 5—DEMAND ESTIMATION

1.   If a regression coefficient passes the t-test, it means that

   a.   the regression equation is valid.
*   b.   the regression coefficient is significantly different from zero.
   c.   the regression coefficient can be used for forecasting.
   d.   the regression coefficient should be included in the regression equation.

2.   Which of the following is a test of the statistical significance of the entire regression equation?

   a.   t-test
   b.   R2
*   c.   F-test
   d.   Durbin-Watson test

3.   Which of the following is a test of the statistical significance of a particular regression coefficient?

*   a.   t-test
   b.   R2
   c.   F-test
   d.   Durbin-Watson test

4.   Which of the following is a measure of the explanatory power of the regression model?

   a.   t-test
*   b.   R2
   c.   F-test
   d.   Durbin-Watson test

5.   When a regression coefficient is significant at the .05 level, it means that

   a.   there is only a five percent chance that there will be an error in a forecast.
   b.   there is 95 percent chance that the regression coefficient is the true population coefficient.
*   c.   there is a five percent chance or less that the estimated coefficient is zero.
   d.   there is a five percent chance or less that the regression coefficient is not the true population coefficient.

Answer questions 6, 7 and 8 on the basis of the information below. (Standard errors in parentheses, $n = 150$.)

$$Q_D = 1000 - \underset{(20)}{50P_A} + \underset{(7)}{10P_B} + \underset{(.04)}{.05I}$$

where Q_D =   quantity demanded of product "A"
   P_A =   price of product "A"
   P_B =   price of a competing product "B"
   I =   per capita income

6.   Using the "rule of 2," which of the following variables can be deemed statistically significant?

*   a. P^A
     b. P^B
     c.   I
     d.   all of the above
     e.   none of the above

7.   If P_A = \$20, P_B = \$18 and I = \$15,000, which of the following statements is true?

     a.   Product A is a superior good.
     b.   Product B is a close competitor of product A.
*   c.   Product A is price elastic.
     d.   All of the above are true.
     e.   None of the above are true.

8.   For which of the following variables should a "two tail" t-test be applied?

     a.   P
*   b.   I
     c.   PC
     d.   should be applied for all.

9.   Which of the following refers to a relatively high correlation among the independent variables of a regression equation?

     a.   autocorrelation
     b.   the identity problem
     c.   statistically insignificant regression coefficients
*   d.   multicollinearity

10.   When the R^2 of a regression equation is very high, it indicates that

     a.   all the coefficients are statistically significant.
     b.   the intercept term has no economic meaning.
*   c.   a high proportion of the variation in the independent variable can be accounted for by the variation in the independent variables.
     d.   there is a good chance of serial correlation and so the equation must be discarded.

11.   The coefficient of a linear regression equation indicates

*   a.   the change in the dependent variable relative to a unit change in the independent variable.
     b.   the change in the independent variable relative to a unit change in the dependent variable.
     c.   the percentage change in the dependent variable relative to a unit change in the independent variable.
     d.   The percentage change in the independent variable relative to a unit change in the dependent variable.

12.   For the regression equation $Q = 100 - 10X_1 + 25X_2$, which of the following statements is true?

   a. X_2 is the more important variable because it is positive.
   b.   When X1 decreases by one unit, Q decreases by 10 units.
   c.   When X1 increases by 10 units, Q decreases by 1 unit.
* d.   When X1 increases by one unit, Q decreases by 10 units.

13.   When using regression analysis for forecasting, the confidence interval indicates:

   a.   the degree of confidence that one has in the equation's R2.
* b.   the range in which the value of the dependent variable is expected to lie with a given degree of probability.
   c.   the degree of confidence that one has in the regression coefficients.
   d.   the range in which the actual outcome of a forecast is going to lie.

14.   Which of the following indicators will always improve when more variables are added to a regression equation?

   a.   the magnitudes of the coefficients
   b.   the t-test
* c.   R2
   d.   the standard errors of the coefficients

15.   Which value from the Durbin-Watson test indicates the least likelihood of serial correlation?

   a.   1
* b.   2
   c.   2
   d.   1

16.   The use of a dummy variable in regression analysis

   a.   indicates that a researchers does not really know what to include in the equation.
* b.   indicates that a variable is expected to either have or not have an impact on a dependent variable.
   c.   indicates that insufficient data is available for the analysis.
   d.   indicates the use of hypothetical data.

17.   In using regression analysis to estimate demand, which of the following problems is most directly a result of insufficient data?

* a.   the identification problem
   b.   the problem of a low R2
   c.   the problem of high standard errors
   d.   the problem of insignificant F-statistics

18.   In the estimation of demand, the "identification problem" refers to

   a.   the problem of selecting the proper level of significance.
   b.   the problem of deciding whether to use time series or cross sectional data.

*   c.   the problem of separating out the effects of price on the quantity demanded when supply cannot be not held constant.

d.   the problem of having insufficient variation in prices.

19.   The t-statistic is computed by

a.   dividing the regression coefficient by the standard error of the estimate.

*   b.   dividing the regression coefficient by the standard error of the coefficient.

c.   dividing the standard error of the coefficient by the regression coefficient.

d.   dividing the R2 by the F-statistic.

20.   Which of the following is most likely to indicate a statistically significant regression coefficient?

a. $t > R2$

b. $R2 > .90$

*   c. $t > 2$

d. $F > 4$

Answer questions 21 through 24 on the basis of the regression results below (standard errors in parentheses, n = 200).

$$Q_D = -500 - 100P_A + 50P_B + .3I + .2A$$
$$\quad\quad (250) \quad\quad (50) \quad\quad (30) \quad\quad (.1) \quad\quad (.08)$$

$$R^2 = .12$$

where Q_D = 10,500, quantity demanded of product "A"

P_A = $10, price of product "A"

P_B = $8, price of product "B"

I = $12,000, per capita income

A = $20,000, monthly advertising expenditure

21.   Which of the variables does not pass the t-test at the .05 level of significance?

a. P_A

*   b. P_B

c.   A

d.   I

e.   all the variables pass the t-test.

22.   As a researcher, which aspect of the results would be of greatest concern?

a.   the negative value of the constant (i.e., -500)

b.   the relatively low impact of the competitor's price

c.   the fact that not all of the variables are statistically significant

*   d.   the poor fit of the regression line

23.   As the manager of Product A, which of the following would be of greatest concern (based on the regression results above)?

    a.   none of the factors below would be of concern.
    b.   an impending recession
 * c.   pressure on you by your salespersons to lower the price so that they can boost their sales
    d.   a price reduction by the makers of product B

24.   Which of the following cannot be determined on the basis of the above regression results?

 * a.   the degree of price elasticity of product B
    b.   whether or not product A is "normal"
    c.   the degree of competition between A and B
    d.   all of the above can be determined.

25.   Which indicator shows how well a regression line fits through the scatter of data points?

    a.   F-test
 * b. R^2
    c.   t-test
    d.   Durbin-Watson test

26.   A dummy variable is also called

    a.   an approximate variable.
 * b.   a discrete variable.
    c.   a zero-sum variable.
    d.   an improper variable.

27.   A manager will have the least confidence in an explanatory variable that:

    a.   does not pass the F-test.
    b.   is expressed as a dummy variable.
 * c.   does not pass the t-test.
    d.   constitutes only a small part of R^2.

28.   From a management policy perspective, which regression result is the most useful?

    a.   a regression equation that passes the F-test
 * b.   a regression equation whose explanatory variables all pass the t-test
    c.   a regression equation that has the highest R^2
    d.   a regression equation that has the least number of dummy variables

CHAPTER 6—FORECASTING

1. (*Qualitative; quantitative) _____ forecasting is based on judgments of individuals or groups while (qualitative; *quantitative) _____ forecasting generally utilizes significant amounts of prior data as a basis for prediction.

2. The fact that a person with a forceful and persuasive personality but not necessarily the greatest amount of knowledge and judgment can exercise a disproportionate amount of influence is a major drawback of

    a. the Delphi method of forecasting.
    b. the market research method.
    c. opinion polling.
    * d. the jury of executive opinion approach.

3. The forecasting technique which predicts technological trends and is carried out by a sequential series of written questions and answers is

    * a. the Delphi method.
    b. the market research method.
    c. opinion polling.
    d. the jury of executive opinion approach.

4. The (lagging; *coincident) _____ indicators identify peaks and troughs of a business cycle, while the (*lagging; coincident) indicators confirm upturns and downturns in economic activity.

5. Average weekly claims for unemployment insurance, money supply and the index of stock prices are all examples of

    * a. leading indicators.
    b. coincident indicators.
    c. lagging indicators.
    d. none of the above.

6. One of the series included among the lagging indicators is

    a. the change in sensitive material prices.
    b. the index of industrial production.
    c. employees on non-agricultural payrolls.
    * d. average duration of unemployment.

7. The following is not one of the leading indicators:

    a. index of consumer expectations, U. of Michigan.
    * b. change in consumer price index for services.
    c. vendor performance, slower deliveries diffusion index.
    d. manufacturers' new orders, nondefense capital goods.

8.   Which of the following is a leading economic indicator?

    a.   Average hours, manufacturing
    b.   Money supply M2
    c.   Stock prices, 500 common stocks
*   d.   All of the above

9.   The method of forecasting with leading indicators can be criticized

    a.   for occasionally forecasting a recession when none ensues.
    b.   for forecasting the direction of the economy but not the size of the change in economic activity.
    c.   for frequent revisions of data after original publication.
*   d.   all of the above.

10.   A general rule of thumb is that if, after a period of increases, the leading indicatorindex sustains _____ consecutive declines, a recession (or at least a slowing of the economy) will follow.

*   a.   three
    b.   four
    c.   five
    d.   six

11.   The forecasting technique which involves the use of the least squares statistical method to examine trends, and takes into account seasonal and cyclical fluctuations, is known as

    a.   compound growth rate projection.
    b.   the Delphi method.
*   c.   time series projection.
    d.   exponential smoothing projection.

12.   Quantitative forecasting that projects past data without explaining the reasons for future trends is called

    a.   scientific forecasting.
    b.   dumb forecasting.
    c.   empirical forecasting.
*   d.   naive forecasting.

13.   The following is not a drawback of forecasting using the compound growth rate method:

    a.   only considers first and last observations.
*   b.   considers only equal absolute changes.
    c.   disregards fluctuations between the original and terminal observations.
    d.   does not consider any trends in the data.

14.   If $1,000 is placed in an account earning 8% annually on January 1, 1999, how much would be in this account on January 1, 2013?

Answer: $2,937

15.   The following are the sales achieved by Jensen Fabrics during the last 7 years:

1993	$116,000
1994	124,000
1995	127,000
1996	146,000
1997	155,000
1998	154,000
1999	162,000

Using the compound growth rate calculation, what would be your estimate for sales in 2000?

Answer: $171,200 (growth rate is 5.7%)

16.   Charting observations on a semi-logarithmic graph will help the analyst to ascertain whether

    a.   absolute changes from period to period are constant.
    b.   whether percentage changes from period to period are constant.
    c.   whether percentage changes from period to period are declining.
*   d.   both b and c.

17.   A major problem in projecting with a trend line is that

    a.   only straight-line projections can be accommodated.
    b.   it is valid only if the trend is upward.
*   c.   it will not forecast turning points in activity.
    d.   it is a very complex method of forecasting.

18.   The following is the exponential trend equation to forecast sales (S):

    a. $S = a + b(t)$
*   b. $S = a + b^t$
    c. $S = a + b(t) + c(t)^2$
    d.   none of the above

19.   You are given the following straight-line trend equation: Sales = 1,275 + 89.3t, where 1990 represents t = 1. Project sales for 2000.

Answer: 2,257.3

20.   Among the advantages of the _____ technique of forecasting are ease of calculation, relatively little requirement for analytical skills, and the ability to provide the analyst with information regarding the statistical significance of results and the size of statistical errors.

*   a.   least-squares trend analysis
    b.   compound growth rate
    c.   visual trend-fitting
    d.   expert opinion

21.   Among the advantages of the least-squares trend analysis techniques is

    a.   the ease of calculation.
    b.   relatively little analytical skill required.
    c.   its ability to provide information regarding the statistical significance of the results.
*   d.   all of the above.

22.   The forecasting method that involves using an average of past observations to predict the future (if the forecaster feels that the future is a reflection of some average of past results) is the

    a.   moving average method.
    b.   econometric forecasting method.
    c.   exponential smoothing method.
    d.   both a. and b.
*   e.   both a. and c.

23.   An explanatory forecasting technique in which the analyst must select independent variables that help determine the dependent variable is called

    a.   exponential smoothing.
*   b.   regression analysis.
    c.   trend analysis.
    d.   moving average method.

24.   When the more recent observations are more relevant to the estimate of the next period than previous observations, the naive forecasting method to employ is

*   a.   exponential smoothing.
    b.   compound growth rate.
    c.   trend analysis.
    d.   moving averages.

25.   The following are the actual sales for the last six periods:

Period	Sales
1	750
2	820
3	600
4	850
5	900
6	700

Using a 3-month moving average, what would be your prediction for period 7?

Answer: 817

26.   The following are the actual sales for the last six periods:

Period	Sales
1	750
2	820
3	600
4	850
5	900
6	700

If the exponential smoothing forecasting method is used, and the smoothing factor is .6, what will be the forecast for period 7?

Answer: 761

27.   The following are the actual sales for the last six periods:

Period	Sales
1	750
2	820
3	600
4	850
5	900
6	700

CHAPTER 7 AND APPENDIXES—THE THEORY AND ESTIMATION OF PRODUCTION

1.   The difference between the short-run and the long-run production function is:

    a.   three months or one business quarter.
*   b.   the time it takes for firms to change all production inputs.
    c.   the time it takes for firms to change only their variable inputs.
    d.   more information is required to answer this question.

2.   A firm using two inputs, X and Y, is using them in the most efficient manner when

    a.   MPX = MPY
    b.   PX = PY and MPX = MPY
    c.   MPX/PY = MPY/PX
*   d.   MPX/MPY = PX/PY

3.   Which of the following is <u>not</u> true about the law of diminishing returns?

    a.   It is a short run phenomenon.
    b.   It refers to diminishing marginal product.
    c.   It will have an impact on the firm's marginal cost.
*   d.   It divides Stage I and II of the production process.
    e.   All of the above are true.

4.   Which of the following indicates when Stage II ends and Stage III begins in the short run production function?

    a.   When AP = 0
*   b.   When MP = 0
    c.   When MP = AP
    d.   when MP starts to diminish

5.   Which of the following indicate when Stage I ends and Stage II begins in the short run production?

    a.   When AP = 0
    b.   When MP = 0
*   c.   When MP = AP
    d.   When MP starts to diminish

6.   Which of the following statements about the short-run production function is true?

    a.   MP always equals AP at the maximum point of MP.
*   b.   MP always equals zero when TP is at its maximum point.
    c.   TP starts to decline at the point of diminishing returns.
    d.   When MP diminishes, AP is at its minimum point.
    e.   None of the above is true.

7. Assume a firm employs 10 workers and pays each $15 per hour. Further assume that the MP of the 10th worker is 5 units of output and that the price of the output is $4. According to economic theory, in the short run,

*   a.   the firm should hire additional workers.
        b.   the firm should reduce the number of workers employed.
        c.   the firm should continue to employ 10 workers.
        d.   more information is required to answer this question.

8. Which of the following is the <u>best</u> example of two inputs that would exhibit a constant marginal rate of technical substitution?

        a.   trucks and truck drivers
*   b.   natural gas and oil
        c.   personal computers and clerical workers
        d.   company employed computer programmers and temporary supplemental computer programmers

9. Decreasing returns to scale

        a.   indicates that an increase in all inputs by some proportion will result in a decrease in output.
        b.   must always occur at some point in the production process.
        c.   is directly related to the law of diminishing returns.
        d.   All of the above are true.
*   e.   None of the above is true.

10. A firm that operates in Stage III of the short run production function

        a.   has too much fixed capacity relative to its variable inputs.
*   b.   has too little fixed capacity relative to its variable inputs.
        c.   has greatly overestimated the demand for its output.
        d.   should try to increase the amount of variable input used.

11. Which of the following combination of inputs is most closely reflective of decreasing marginal rate of technical substitution (MRTS)?

        a.   oil and natural gas
        b.   sugar and high fructose corn syrup
*   c.   computers and clerks
        d.   keyboards and computers

12. In the short run, finding the optimal amount of variable input involves which relationship?

        a.   MP = MC
        b.   AP = MP
        c.   MP = 0
*   d.   MRP = MFC

13.   The perfect substitution of two inputs implies that

    a.   two inputs can be substituted at a ratio of 1 to 1.
    b.   one input can be substituted for another up to some point.
*   c.   two inputs can be substituted at some constant ratio.
    d.   one input can be substituted for another.

14.   If a firm finds itself operating in Stage I, it implies that

    a.   variable inputs are extremely expensive.
*   b.   it overinvested in fixed capacity.
    c.   it underinvested in fixed capacity.
    d.   fixed inputs are extremely expensive.

15.   If MRP > MLC, it means that a firm should

    a.   use less labor.
*   b.   use more labor.
    c.   increase its fixed capacity.
    d.   decrease its fixed capacity.

16.   In the long run, a firm is said to be experiencing <u>decreasing</u> returns to scale if a 10 percent increase in inputs results in

    a.   an increase in output from 100 to 110.
    b.   a decrease in output from 100 to 90.
*   c.   an increase in output from 100 to 105.
    d.   a decrease in output from 100 to 85.

17.   When is it <u>not</u> in the best interest of a company to hire additional workers in the short run?

    a.   when the average product of labor is decreasing
    b.   when the firm is in Stage II of the production process
    c.   when the marginal revenue product equals zero
*   d.   when the wage rate is equal to or greater than labor's marginal revenue product

18.   When the law of diminishing returns takes effect

*   a.   firms must add increasingly more input if they are to maintain the same extra amount of output.
    b.   firms must add decreasingly more input if they are to maintain the same extra amount of output.
    c.   more input must be added in order to increase its output.
    d.   a firm must always try to add the same amount of input to the production process.

19.   An isoquant indicates

    a.   different combinations of two inputs that can be purchased for the same amount of money.
*   b.   different combinations of two inputs that can produce the same amount of output.
    c.   different combinations of output that can be produced with the same amount of input.
    d.   different combinations of output that cost the same amount to produce.

20. If a firm used a combination of inputs that was to the left of its isocost line, it would indicate that

    a. it is exceeding its budget.
*   b. it is not spending all of its budget.
    c. it is operating at its optimal point because it is saving money.
    d. none of the above.

Answer Questions 21, 22, and 23 on the basis of the data below.

Input	TP	AP	MP	TRP	MRP	TLC	MLC
0	0		0	0		0	
1	10000	10000	10000	25000	25000	9000	9000
2	25000	12500	15000	62500	37500	18000	9000
3	45000	15000	20000	112500	50000	27000	9000
4	60000	15000	15000	150000	37500	36000	9000
5	70000	14000	10000	175000	25000	45000	9000
6	75000	12500	5000	187500	12500	54000	9000
7	78000	11143	3000	195000	7500	63000	9000
8	80000	10000	2000	200000	5000	72000	9000

21. The law of diminishing returns begins when the _____ unit of output is produced.

Answer: 4th

22. Output level 7500 lies in what stage of the production process? _____

Answer: Stage II

23. The optimal number of labor inputs to use is _____?

Answer: 6

24. In economic theory, if an additional worker adds less to the total output than previous workers hired, it is because

*   a. there may be less that this person can do, given the fixed capacity of the firm.
    a. he/she is less skilled than the previously hired workers.
    b. everyone is getting in each other's way.
    c. the firm is experiencing diminishing returns to scale.

25. In a call center, which of the following could be considered to be a variable input in the short run?

    a. the level of computer-telephony software being utilized
*   b. the number of call center representatives on duty at the center
    c. the number of call center managers or supervisors
    d. the size (e.g., square footage) of the call center

26.   A major advantage of the _____ production function is that it can be easily transformed into a linear function, and thus can be analyzed with the linear regression method.

    a. cubic
*   b. power
    c. quadratic
    d. none of the above

27.   _____ functions are very useful in an analyzing production functions which exhibit both increasing and decreasing marginal products.

    a. Cobb-Douglas
    b. straight-line
    c. quadratic
*   d. cubic

28.   The following equation has been derived from a _____ total production function:
$$MP = b + 2cV - 3dV^2$$
*   a. cubic
    b. quadratic
    c. power
    d. linear

29.   The following Cobb-Douglas production function,
$$Q = 1.8L^{0.74}K^{0.36}$$
exhibits

*   a. increasing returns.
    b. constant returns.
    c. decreasing returns.
    d. both a. and b.

30.   Given the following production function,
$$Q = 7V + .6V^2 - .1V^3,$$
calculate total quantity, average product and marginal product when V = 6.

Answers: 42, 7, 3.4

31.   The following is not one of the strengths of the Cobb-Douglas production function:

    a. both marginal product and returns to scale can be estimated from it.
    b. it can be converted into a linear function for ease of calculation.
*   c. it shows a production function passing through increasing returns to constant returns and then to decreasing returns.
    d. the sum of the exponents indicates whether returns to scale are increasing, constant or decreasing.

32. When seven units of a variable factor used, total plant production is 44.1 units. Marginal product at this point is .7. The elasticity of production is

   a. 6.3.
*   b. 0.11.
   c. 9.
   d. 0.143.

33. An advantage of using the cross-sectional regression method in estimating production is that

*   a. the problem of technological change over time is overcome.
   b. there is no need to adjust data which are in monetary terms for geographical differences.
   c. we can assume that all plants operate at their most efficient input combinations.
   d. all of the above.

34. When the exponents of a Cobb-Douglas production function sum to more than 1, the function exhibits

   a. constant returns.
*   b. increasing returns.
   c. decreasing returns.
   d. either increasing or decreasing returns.

CHAPTER 8 AND APPENDIXES—THE THEORY AND ESTIMATION OF COST

1. Which of the following cost functions indicates that the law of diminishing returns takes effect as soon as production begins?

  * a. $1000 + 2.5Q + .05Q2$
     b. $1000 + 2.5Q$
     c. $1000 + 2.5Q - 1.2Q2 + .03Q3$
     d. Not enough information to determine this

2. Which of the following relationships is correct?

     a. When marginal product starts to decrease, marginal cost starts to decrease.
     b. When marginal cost starts to increase, average cost starts to increase.
     c. When marginal cost starts to increase, average variable cost starts to increase.
  * d. When marginal product starts to decrease, marginal cost starts to increase.

3. The law of diminishing returns begins first to affect a firm's short-run cost structure when

     a. average variable cost begins to increase.
  * b. marginal cost begins to increase.
     c. average cost begins to increase.
     d. average fixed cost begins to decrease.

4. Which of the following statements best represents a difference between short-run and long-run cost?

     a. Less than one year is considered the short run; more than one year the long run.
  * b. there are no fixed costs in the long run.
     c. in the short run labor must always be considered the variable input and capital the fixed input.
     d. all of the above are true.

5. The relationship between MC and AC can best be described as follows

     a. when AC increases, MC starts to increase.
     b. when MC increases, AC starts to increase.
     c. when MC decreases, AC decreases.
  * d. when MC exceeds AC, AC starts to increase.

6. Average fixed cost is

  * a. AC minus AVC.
     b. TC divided by Q.
     c. AVC minus MC.
     d. TC minus TVC.

7. Which of the following cost relationships is <u>not</u> true?

  * a. AFC = AC - MC
     b. TVC = TC - TFC

c.   the change in TVC/the change in Q = MC
d.   the change in TC/ the change in Q = MC

8.   Economists consider which of the following costs to be <u>irrelevant</u> to a short-run business decision?

   a.   opportunity cost
   b.   out-of-pocket cost
* c.   historical cost
   d.   replacement cost

9.   Which of the following is a relevant cost?

* a.   replacement cost
   b.   sunk cost
   c.   historical cost
   d.   fixed cost
   e.   all of the above are relevant.

10.   Which of the following is a reason for economies of scale?

   a.   fixed costs are spread out as volume increases.
   b.   the law of diminishing returns does not take effect.
* c.   input productivity increases as a result of greater specialization.
   d.   there is greater savings in transportation costs.

11.   Diseconomies of scale can be caused by

   a.   the law of diminishing returns.
* b.   bureaucratic inefficiencies.
   c.   increasing advertising and promotional costs.
   d.   all of the above.

12.   When a firm increased its output by one unit, its AC rose from $45 to $50. This implies that its MC is

   a. $5.
   b.   between $45 and $50.
* c.   greater than $50.
   d.   cannot be determined from the above information.

13.   When a firm increased its output by one unit, its AC decreased. This implies that

* a.   MC < AC.
   b.   MC = AC.
   c.   MC < AFC.
   d.   The law of diminishing returns has not yet taken effect.

14.   When a firm increased its output by unit, its AFC decreased. This is an indication that

   a.   the law of diminishing returns has taken effect.
   b.   MC < AFC.

    c. AVC < AFC.
*   d. the firm is spreading out its total fixed cost.

15.   The main factor that explains the difference between accounting cost and economic cost is

*   a. opportunity cost.
    b. fixed cost.
    c. variable cost.
    d. all of the above help to explain the difference.

16.   Economies of scale is indicated by

    a. declining long run AVC.
    b. declining long run AFC.
*   c. declining long run AC.
    d. declining long run TC.

17.   Which of the following distinctions helps to explain the difference between relevant and irrelevant cost?

    a. accounting cost vs. direct cost
*   b. historical cost vs. replacement cost
    c. sunk cost vs. fixed cost
    d. variable cost vs. incremental cost

18.   Which of the following distinctions <u>does not</u> help to explain the difference between relevant and irrelevant cost?

    a. historical vs. replacement cost
    b. sunk vs. incremental cost
    c. variable vs. fixed cost
*   d. out-of-pocket vs. opportunity cost
    e. all help to explain the difference

19.   Which of the following actions has the <u>best</u> potential for experiencing economies of scope?

    a. producing a product that has appeal to a wider segment of the market
    b. producing computers and software
    c. producing spaghetti and soft drinks
*   d. producing cars and trucks

20.   The learning curve indicates that

    a. economies of scale is taking effect.
*   b. repetition of various production tasks cause unit costs to decrease.
    c. workers must learn new skills in order to improve.
    d. it takes time to learn a new skill.

21. When a firm's MC curve shifts to the right, it implies that

    a. new firms are entering the market.
    b. labor productivity is decreasing.
*   c. labor productivity is increasing.
    d. the firm's overhead costs are decreasing.

22. When a firm experiences increasing returns to scale

    a. its AFC will decrease.
    b. its AFC will increase.
    c. its AC will increase.
*   d. its AC will decrease.

23. If a firm's rent increases, it will affect its cost structure in the following way:

    a. AVC will increase.
    b. MC will increase.
*   c. TFC will increase.
    d. all of the above will increase.

24. Assuming the existence of economies of scale, if a firm finds that it can reduce its unit cost by <u>decreasing</u> its scale of production, it means that

*   a. it has too much production capacity relative to its demand.
    b. it should try to produce less.
    c. the law of diminishing returns has not taken effect.
    d. it has too much fixed overhead relative to its variable cost.

25. Which of the following relationships implies that a firm's short run cost function is linear?

    a. MC = AC
*   b. MC = AVC
    c. AC = AFC + AVC
    d. MC > AC

26. The marginal cost will intersect the average variable cost curve

    a. when the average variable cost curve is rising.
    b. where average variable cost curve equals price.
*   c. at the minimum point of the average variable cost curve.
    d. the two will never intersect.

27. Which of the following cost functions will exhibit both decreasing and increasing marginal costs?

*   a. a cubic cost function
    b. a quadratic cost function
    c. a linear cost function
    d. all of the above

28.   If total cost equals $2,000 and quantity produced is 100 units,

     a.   then fixed cost is $200 and average variable cost is $18.
     b.   then fixed cost is $600 and average variable cost is $14,
     c.   then fixed cost is $500 and marginal cost is $15.
*   d.   then either a. or b. can be correct.

29.   The learning curve

     a.   is really no different from a marginal cost curve.
     b.   calculates average cost at a particular point in time.
*   c.   shows the decrease in unit cost as more of the same product is produced over time.
     d.   none of the above.

30.   Which level indicates the point of maximum economic efficiency?

*   a.   lowest point on AC curve
     b.   lowest point on AVC curve
     c.   lowest point on MC curve
     d.   none of the above

31.   MC increases because

     a.   MC naturally increases as firm nears capacity.
     b.   labor is paid overtime wages when volume increases.
     c.   in the short run, MC always increases.
*   d.   the law of diminishing returns takes effect.

32.   Which of the following is the best example of economies of scope?

     a.   Coca-Cola expands its global operations to sub-Sahara Africa.
     b.   alcohol for car fuel is produced from corn.
*   c.   Amazon.com decides to rent out its Web site to independent e-commerce companies.
     d.   a company reduces its cost by getting bigger discounts for bulk purchases.

33.   The distinction between sunk and incremental costs is most helpful in answering which question?

     a.   how many more people should be added to the production process?
     b.   what is the correct price to charge?
     c.   should we begin to build a new factory?
*   d.   should we continue developing a new software application that we began last year?

34.   One of the major strengths of (*cross-sectional; time series) cost estimation is that adjusting the various costs for inflation or other price changes is not necessary.

35.   The results of many empirical studies of short-run cost functions have shown that total costs conform to a

     a.   quadratic total cost function .
     b.   a power cost function.

*   c. a linear cost function.
     d. a cubic cost function.

36. Among the problems encountered when time series analysis is used to estimate cost functions is

     a. that technological changes may have occurred.
     b. that accounting changes may have occurred during the period analyzed.
     c. that some costs are recorded on the books of account at a time other than when they are incurred.
*   d. all of the above.

37. The method of estimating long-run costs in which knowledgeable professionals familiar with production facilities and processes calculate optimal combination of inputs to produce given quantities and then estimate costs is known as

*   a. engineering cost estimating.
     b. the survivorship method.
     c. regression analysis.
     d. none of the above.

38. When the survivorship method of cost estimating is used, an increase, over time, in the proportion of industry product produced by medium size firms indicates the existence of

     a. continuing economies of scale.
     b. continuing diseconomies of to scale.
*   c. a U-shaped long-run average cost curve.
     d. large technological changes.

39. The major advantages of using cross-sectional analysis for long-run costs studies include

     a. the inclusion in the sample of different plants of different sizes.
     b. the avoidance of having to adjust for inflationary trends.
     c. the avoidance of having to account for interregional cost differences.
     d. all of the above.
*   e. a. and b. above.

40. A short-run total cost function of the following form:
$$TC = 100 + 32Q - 4Q^2 + 0.4Q^3,$$
     indicates the existence of

     a. a linear total cost curve.
     b. a constant average variable cost curve.
*   c. a U-shaped average total cost curve.
     d. a constant marginal cost curve.

CHAPTER 9—PRICING AND OUTPUT DECISIONS: PERFECT COMPETITION AND MONOPOLY

1.   Which of the following products is the best example of perfect competition:

      a.   automobiles
*   b.   apples
      c.   soap
      d.   video cassettes

2.   Which of the following is not characteristic of perfect competition?

*   a.   a differentiated product
      b.   no barriers to entry or exit
      c.   large number of buyers
      d.   complete knowledge of market price

3.   Which of the following conditions would definitely cause a perfectly competitive company to shut down in the short run?

      a. $P < MC$
      b. $P = MC < AC$
*   c. $P < AVC$
      d. $P = MR$

4.   In economic analysis, any amount of profit earned above zero is considered "above normal" because

      a.   normally firms are supposed to earn zero profit.
*   b.   this would indicate that the firm's revenue exceeded both its accounting and opportunity cost.
      c.   this would indicate that the firm was at least earning a profit equal to its opportunity cost.
      d.   this would indicate that the firm's revenue exceeded its accounting cost.

5.   If a perfectly competitive firm incurs an economic loss, it should

      a.   shut down immediately.
      b.   try to raise its price.
      c.   shut down in the long run.
*   d.   shut down if this loss exceeds fixed cost.

6.   At the point at which P=MC, suppose that a perfectly competitive firm's MC = $100, its AVC = $80 and its AC = $110. This firm should

      a.   shut down immediately.
*   b.   continue operating in the short run.
      c.   try to take advantage of economies of scale.
      d.   try to increase its advertising and promotion.

7. A perfectly competitive firm sells 15 units of output at the going market price of $10. Suppose its average cost is $15 and its average variable cost is $8. Its contribution margin (i.e., contribution to fixed cost) is

*   a. $30.
     b. $150.
     c. $105.
     d. cannot be determined from the above information.

8. When a firm produces at the point where MR = MC, the profit that it is earning is considered to be

     a. maximum.
     b. normal.
     c. above normal.
*   d. not enough information is provided.

9. When a firm has the power to establish its price,

     a. P = MR
     b. P = MC
*   c. P > MR
     d. P < MR

10. When MR = MC,

     a. marginal profit is maximized.
*   b. total profit is maximized.
     c. marginal profit is positive.
     d. total profit is zero.

11. In the short run, which of the following would indicate that a perfectly competitive firm is producing an output for which it is receiving a normal profit?

     a. P > AC
     b. AVC < P < AC
*   c. P = AC
     d. P = AVC

12. A firm that seeks to maximize its revenue is most likely to adhere to which of the following?

     a. MR = MC
*   b. MR = 0
     c. MR = P
     d. MR < MC

13. Which of the following is true for a monopoly?

     a. P = MC
     b. P = MR
*   c. P > MR
     d. P < MR

14. Which of the following characteristics is most important in differentiating between perfect competition and all other types of markets?

    a. whether or not the product is standardized
    b. whether or not there is complete market information about price
*   c. whether or not firms are price takers
    d. all of the above are equally important.

15. Suppose a firm is currently maximizing its profits (i.e., following the MR=MC rule). Assuming that it wants to continue maximizing its profits, if its fixed costs increase, it should

*   a. maintain the same price.
    b. raise its price.
    c. lower its price.
    d. not enough information to answer this question.

16. Suppose a firm is currently maximizing its profits (i.e., following the MR=MC rule). Assuming it wants to continue maximizing its profits, if its variable costs decrease, it should

*   a. lower its price in response to the lower costs.
    b. raise its price in order to earn more profits.
    c. maintain the same price.
    d. not enough information to answer this question.

17. Which of the following is true about a monopoly?

*   a. its demand curve is generally less elastic than in more competitive markets.
    b. it will always earn economic profit.
    c. it will try to charge the highest possible price.
    d. it will always be subject to government regulation.
    e. none of the above is true.

18. Assume a profit maximizing firm's short run cost is $TC = 700 + 60Q$. If its demand curve is $P = 300 - 15Q$, what should it do in the short run?

    a. shut down
    b. continue operating in the short run even though it is losing money
*   c. continue operating because it is earning an economic profit
    d. cannot be determined from the above information

19. Assume a perfectly competitive firm's short run cost is $TC = 100 + 160Q + 3Q2$. If the market price is \$196, what should it do?

    a. produce 5 units and continue operating
*   b. produce 6 units and continue operating
    c. produce zero units (i.e., shut down)
    d. cannot be determined from the above information

Answer questions 20, 21, and 22 on the basis of the numerical example below.

Quantity	Price	Marginal Revenue	Average Fixed Cost	Average Variable Cost	Average Total Cost	Marginal Cost
0	152					
1	142	142	100.00	138.30	238.30	138.30
2	132	122	50.00	124.20	174.20	110.10
3	122	102	33.33	112.70	146.03	89.70
4	112	82	25.00	103.80	128.80	77.10
5	102	62	20.00	97.50	117.50	72.30
6	92	42	16.67	93.80	110.47	75.30
7	82	22	14.29	92.70	106.99	86.10
8	72	2	12.50	94.20	106.70	104.70
9	62	-18	11.11	98.30	109.41	131.10
10	52	-38	10.00	105.00	115.00	165.30

20. Assuming this firm is a short run profit maximizer or loss minimizer, which statement best describes its present situation?

    a. It should shut down immediately.
*   b. It is incurring a loss but should continue operating in the short run.
    c. It is earning a only a normal profit.
    d. It is earning above normal profit.
    e. Insufficient data to answer this question.

21. Suppose this firm is operating in a perfectly competitive market as price taker. If the market price is $90, in the short run, this firm should

    a. produce 8 units of output.
    b. produce 9 units of output.
    c. produce 7 units of output.
*   d. produce 0 units of output (i.e., shut down).
    e. insufficient information to answer this question.

22. This same price taking firm would be earning an economic profit as long as the market price is greater than

*   a. $72.30.
    b. $106.70.
    c. $92.70.
    d. Insufficient information to answer this question.

23. A monopoly will usually produce

    a. where its demand curve is inelastic.
*   b. where its demand curve is elastic.
    c. where its demand curve is either elastic or inelastic.
    d. only when its demand curve is perfectly inelastic.

24. The main difference between the price-quantity graph of a perfectly competitive firm and a monopoly is

* a. that the competitive firm's demand curve is horizontal, while that of the monopoly is downward sloping.
   b. that a monopoly always earns an economic profit while a competitive company always earns only normal profit.
   c. that a monopoly maximizes its profit when marginal revenue is greater than marginal cost.
   d. that a monopoly does not incur increasing marginal cost.

25. When the slope of the total revenue curve is equal to the slope of the total cost curve

   a. monopoly profit is maximized.
   b. marginal revenue equals marginal cost.
   c. the marginal cost curve intersects the total average cost curve.
   d. the total cost curve is at its minimum.
* e. both a. and b.

CHAPTER 10—PRICING AND OUTPUT DECISIONS: MONOPOLISTIC COMPETITION AND OLIGOPOLY

1.   Oligopoly may be associated with all of the following except

*   a.   many firms.
     b.   a standardized product.
     c.   advertising.
     d.   price followers.
     e.   a. and b.

2.   If firms are earning economic profit in a monopolistically competitive market, which of the following is most likely to happen in the long run?

     a.   some firms will leave the market
     b.   firms will join together to keep others from entering
*   c.   new firms will enter the market, thereby eliminating the economic profit
     d.   firms will continue to earn economic profit

3.   Mutual interdependence means that

     a.   all firms are price takers.
*   b.   each firm sets its own price based on its anticipated reaction by its competitors.
     c.   all firms collaborate to establish one price.
     d.   all firms are free to enter or leave the market.

4.   In which of these markets would the firms be facing the least elastic demand curve?

     a.   perfect competition
*   b.   pure monopoly
     c.   monopolistic competition
     d.   oligopoly

5.   In the long run, the most helpful action that a monopolistically competitive firm can take to maintain its economic profit is to

*   a.   continue its efforts to differentiate its product.
     b.   raise its price.
     c.   lower its price.
     d.   do nothing, because it will inevitably experience a decline in profits.

6.   If an oligopolistic firm decides to raise its price,

     a.   other firms will automatically follow.
     b.   none of the other firms will follow.
*   c.   other firms may follow if it is the price leader.
     d.   only some of the firms will follow.

7.   The main difference between perfect competition and monopolistic competition is

     a.   the number of sellers in the market.
     b.   the ease of exit from the market.
     c.   the degree of information about market price.
*   d.   the degree of product differentiation.

8.   The demand curve which assumes that competitors will follow price decreases but not price increases is called

     a   an industry demand curve.
     b.   an inelastic demand curve.
*   c.   a kinked demand curve.
     d.   a competitive demand curve.

9.   The existence of a kinked demand curve under oligopoly conditions may result in

     a.   price flexibility.
*   b.   price rigidity.
     c.   competitive pricing.
     d.   none of the above.

10. When a company is faced by a kinked demand curve, the marginal revenue curve

     a.   will be upward sloping.
     b.   will be horizontal.
     c.   will always be zero at the quantity produced.
*   d.   will be discontinuous.

11. Porter's "Five Forces" Model is based on

     a.   the laws of supply and demand.
     b.   the law of diminishing returns.
*   c.   the Structure-Conduct-Performance model.
     d.   the key factors affecting demand.

12. The four-firm concentration ratio

     a.   indicates the total profitability among the top four firms in an industry.
     b.   is an indicator of the degree of monopolistic competition.
*   c.   indicates the presence and intensity of an oligopoly market.
     d.   is used by the government as a basis for anti-trust cases.

CHAPTER 11—BREAK-EVEN ANALYSIS

1.   Break-even analysis usually assumes all of the following except:

*   a.   in the short run, there is no distinction between variable and fixed costs.
       b.   revenue and cost curve are straight-line throughout the analysis.
       c.   there appears to be perfect competition since the price is considered to remain the same regardless of quantity.
       d.   the straight-line cost curve implies that marginal cost is constant.

2.   An increase in fixed cost will

       a.   decrease the break-even quantity point.
*   b.   increase the break-even quantity point.
       c.   will be offset by an increase in price.
       d.   will have no effect on the analysis.

3.   The break-even quantity point will decrease, when

       a.   variable cost per unit increases.
       b.   fixed cost decreases.
       c.   price increases.
*   d.   both b. and c. above.

4.   In order to find the quantity which must be produced when a certain amount of profit is required per period, the basic break-even formula must be adjusted by

       a.   adding the required profit to the variable cost.
       b.   deducting the required profit from revenue.
*   c.   adding the required profit to fixed cost.
       d.   none of the above.

5.   In order to find the quantity which must be produced when a specific profit per unit is required, the basic break-even formula must be adjusted by

       a.   adding the required unit profit to average variable cost.
       b.   subtracting the required unit profit from price.
       c.   adding the required profit to fixed cost.
*   d.   both a. and b. above.

6.   In break-even analysis, there is usually (*one; more than one) _____ quantity at which there is no profit, while in the usual short-run economic analysis, there is/are usually (one; *two) quantity(ies) _____ at which there is no profit, and profit is maximized (*between the two quantities; at higher quantities; at lower quantities) _____.

7. If the unit price is $7, the variable cost per unit is $4, and the fixed cost per period is $60,000, the quantity at which the company will break even will be

    a. 10,000.
    b. 15,000.
*   c. 20,000.
    d. 25,000.

8. If a company wants to break even at 20,000 units, its variable cost per unit is $3, and its fixed cost per period is $40,000, its selling price per unit will have to be

*   a. $5.
    b. $5.50.
    c. $6.
    d. $6.50.

9. A company sells 20,000 units of its product per period at $10 per unit, while its fixed cost is $100,000 per period. In order to break even, its variable cost per unit cannot exceed

    a. $6.
    b. $5.50.
*   c. $5.
    d. $4.50.

The following data are to be utilized for questions 10 through 13.

Floyd's Coffee Shop collects on the average $8 per customer. Its variable cost per customer averages $5, and its annual fixed cost is $60,000.

10. In order to break even, it must serve _____ customers per year.

    Answers: 20,000

11. If Floyd wants to make a profit of $20,000 per year, it will have to serve _____ customer per year.

    Answer: 26,667

12. If Floyd serves 30,000 customers per year, its profit will be _____.

    Answer: $30,000

13. If Floyd serves 25,000 customers per year, the degree of operating leverage is _____.

    Answer: 5

14. The degree of operating leverage can be defined as

  a. the change in profit for a $1 change in quantity.
  b. the change in quantity for a $1 change in profit.
  c. the percentage change in quantity for a given percentage change in profit.
* d. the percentage change in profit for a given percentage change in quantity.

15. A high degree of operating leverage will

* a. cause a company's profit to fluctuate more widely as sales revenue changes.
  b. cause a company's profit to fluctuate less widely as sales revenue changes.
  c. cause profits to be high.
  d. cause profits to be low.

16. At the break-even point, degree of operating leverage

  a. is at its highest point.
  b. is at its lowest point.
* c. cannot be defined.
  d. none of the above

17. For a given percentage change in sales, the higher the degree of operating leverage,

* a. the higher will be the percentage change in profit.
  b. the lower will be the percentage change in profit.
  c. the higher will be the absolute change in profit.
  d. the lower will be the absolute change in profit.

The following information is to be used in answering questions 18 through 22.

  Company A sells its product for $4 per unit, has variable costs per unit of $2.50, and its fixed cost is $50,000 per period.

  Company B sells a product similar to A's for $3.80 per unit, has variable costs per unit of $1.80, and its fixed cost is $80,000 per period.

18. The break-even quantity for A is _____, and for B is _____.

  Answers: 33,333, 40,000

19. The break-even revenue for A is _____, and for B is _____.

  Answers: $133,333, $152,000

20. The two companies will have the same profit when the production for each reaches _____ units, and the amount of profit for each will be _____.

  Answers: 60,000, $40,000

21. At the quantity produced in question 18, the degree of operating leverage for A will be _____, and for B it will be _____.

Answers: 2.25, 3

22. If production reaches 70,000 units per period, then

      a. A's profit will be higher than B's.
 *   b. B's profit will be higher than A's.
      c. both will earn the same profit.
      d. cannot tell which will make the higher profit.

23. If a company's annual fixed cost is $80,000 and the variable cost is 70% of total revenue, the break-even annual revenue will be _____.

Answer: $266,667

24. If in question 23, the company wants to achieve an annual profit of $40,000, the its annual revenue must be _____.

Answer: $400,000

25. All of the following are limitations of break-even analysis except:

      a. the analysis does not result in identification of a maximum profit point.
      b. in order to use break even analysis, only one product can be produced in a given plant, or if there are several products, their mix must remain fairly constant.
      c. it assumes the existence of linear relationships, constant prices and average variable costs.
      d. it is assumed that costs (and expenses) are either fixed or variable.
 *   e. all of the above are limitations of break-even analysis.

26. Break-even analysis is useful in all the following cases, except:

      a. the calculation of alternative cases when time is of the essence.
      b. the making of small, quick corrections.
      c. in the early stages of a product plan, when few details are available.
 *   d. to prepare a detailed, "bottom-up" plan.

CHAPTER 12—SPECIAL PRICING PRACTICES

1. All of the following are conditions which are favorable to the formation of cartels, except:

   a. the existence of a small number of firms.
   b. geographic proximity of firms.
   c. homogeneity of the product.
   * d. easy entry into the industry.
   e. all of the above conditions are favorable to the formation of cartels.

2. Prices under an ideal cartel situation will be equal to

   * a. monopoly prices.
   b. competitive prices.
   c. prices under monopolistic competition.
   d. marginal cost.

3. A cartel price will be established at the quantity where

   a. total cost equals the industry total revenue.
   b. average cost equals the industry revenue.
   * c. the sum of the members' marginal costs equals industry marginal revenue.
   d. marginal cost equals industry price.

4. Cartel agreements tend to break down

   a. during economic downturns.
   b. because of price "chiseling" by one or more members.
   c. when there is overcapacity in the industry.
   * d. because of all of the above.

5. Barometric price leadership exists when

   * a. one firm in the industry initiates a price change and the others may or may not follow.
   b. one firm imposes its best price on the rest of the industry.
   c. when all firms agree to change prices simultaneously.
   d. when one company forms a price umbrella for all others.

6. Dominant price leadership exists when

   a. one firm drives the others out of the market.
   b. the dominant firm decides how much each of its competitors can sell.
   * c. the dominant firm establishes the price at the quantity where its MR = MC, and permits all other firms to sell all they want to sell at that price.
   d. the dominant firm charges the lowest price in the industry.

7. Dominant price leadership tends to break down

   a. as markets grow and new firms enter the industry.
   b. as technology changes.

    c.   when the dominant firm decides to make the industry more competitive.

*   d.   both a. and b. above.

8.   The oligopolistic situation in which a company's objective is to maximize revenue subject to a minimum profit requirement is usually referred to as

       a.   the aggregate model.

*   b.   the Baumol model.

       c.   the aggressive model.

       d.   the Marshall model.

9.   In the Baumol model, the total quantity sold will usually be larger than

       a.   if perfect competition prevailed.

       b.   if total costs were minimized.

*   c.   if profit were maximized.

       d.   if companies were interdependent.

10.   In the Baumol model, a change in fixed costs will

       a.   increase total quantity sold.

       b.   have no effect on total quantity sold.

       c.   decrease total quantity sold.

*   d.   have an effect on total quantity sold.

11.   Price discrimination exists when

       a.   two different sellers charge different prices for the same product.

       b.   one company sells identical products in different markets at different prices.

       c.   the ratio of price to marginal cost differs for similar products.

*   d.   both b. and c. above.

12.   In order that price discrimination can exist,

       a.   markets must be capable of being separated.

       b.   markets must be interdependent.

       c.   different demand price elasticities must exist in different markets.

       d.   demand price elasticities must be identical in all markets.

*   e.   both a. and c.

13.   Third-degree price discrimination exists when

       a.   the seller knows exactly how much each potential customer is willing to pay and will charge accordingly.

       b.   different prices are charged by blocks of services.

*   c.   when the seller can separate markets by geography, income, age, etc., and charge different prices to these different groups.

       d.   when the seller will bargain with buyers in each of the markets to obtain the best possible price.

14. The result for the seller of being able to practice price discrimination will be

*   a. higher profits.
     b. lower demand elasticity.
     c. lower quantity sold.
     d. cost minimization.

15. The practice by a monopolist of charging each buyer the highest price he/she is willing to pay is called

*   a. first-degree discrimination.
     b. second-degree discrimination.
     c. third-degree discrimination.
     d. fourth-degree discrimination.

16. When state universities charge higher tuition fees to out-of-state students than to local students, the universities are practicing

     a. first-degree discrimination.
     b. second-degree discrimination.
*   c. third-degree discrimination.
     d. fourth-degree discrimination.

17. The following are possible examples of price discrimination, except:

     a. prices in export markets are lower than for identical products in the domestic market.
     b. senior citizens pay lower fares on public transportation than younger people at the same time.
*   c. a product sells at a higher price at location A than at location B, because transportation costs are higher from the factory to A.
     d. subscription prices for a professional journal are higher when bought by a library than when bought by an individual.

18. A tying arrangement exists when

     a. a company sells two products that are substitutes for one another.
     b. a company requires that a customer tie itself down by signing a long-term purchasing agreement.
*   c. a buyer is required to buy both a specific product and its complementary product from the same supplier.
     d. a company offers discounts to customers if they are willing to buy two different products.

19. Under conditions of first-degree price discrimination

*   a. production may equal that which would exist under perfect competition.
     b. production may exceed that which would prevail under perfect competition.
     c. prices will be lower than under perfect competition.
     d. production will always be lower than under perfect competition.

20.   If a product which costs $8 is sold at $10, the profit margin is

      a. $2.
      b.   25%.
*   c.   20%.
      d.   none of the above.

21.   If a product which costs $8 is sold at $10, the mark-up is

      a. $2.
*   b.   25%.
      c.   20%.
      d.   none of the above.

22.   The correct expression for cost plus pricing is

      a.   Price = Cost (1 + profit margin).
      b.   Price = Cost + profit margin.
*   c.   Price = Cost (1 + mark-up).
      d.   Price = Cost + (1 + mark-up).

23.   If the demand elasticity for a product is -2, and a profit-maximizing firm sells the product for $10, its marginal cost must be

*   a. $5.
      b. $10.
      c. $15.
      d. $8.

24.   When mark-up equals 50%, then demand elasticity will be

      a.   -1.
      b.   -1.5.
      c.   -2.
*   d.   -3.

25.   The pricing of a product at each stage of production as the product moves through several stages is called

*   a.   transfer pricing.
      b.   cost plus pricing.
      c.   penetration pricing.
      d.   monopolistic pricing.

26.   A company which charges a lower price than may be indicated by economic analysis to gain a foothold in the market is practicing

      a.   price skimming.
      b.   psychological pricing.
*   c.   penetration pricing.
      d.   prestige pricing.

27. Assume that a multinational company produces components in country A, and ships them to a subsidiary in country B. In order to increase its profits,

*   a. the company should charge a high transfer price for the components if income taxes in country B are higher than in country A.
   b. the company should charge a low transfer price for the components if income taxes in country B are higher than in country A.
   c. the company should charge a high transfer price for the components if income taxes in country A are higher than in country B.
   d. none of the above.

28. A firm in an oligopolistic industry has the following demand and total cost equations:
   $$p = 600 - 20Q$$
   $$TC = 700 + 160Q + 15Q2$$
Calculate

   a. quantity at which profit is maximized.
   b. maximum profit.
   c. quantity at which revenue is maximized.
   d. maximum revenue.
   e. maximum quantity at which profit will be at least $580.
   f. maximum revenue at which profit will be at least $580.

   Answers:

   If revenue and cost schedules are calculated:
   a. 6   b. 680   c. 15   d. 4500   e. 8   f. 3520

   If results are calculated with equations:
   a. 6.286   b. 682.86   c. 15   d. 4500   e. 8   f. 3520

29. A monopolistic firm operates in two separate markets. No trade is possible between market A and market B. The firm has calculated the demand functions for each market as follows:

   Market A $p = 15 - Q$
   Market B $p = 11 - Q$

   The company estimates its total cost function to be
   $$TC = 4Q$$
   Calculate

   a. quantity, total revenue and profit when the company maximizes its profit and charges the same price in both markets.
   b. quantity, total revenue and profit when the company charges different prices in each market and maximizes its total profit.

Answers:

If revenue and cost schedules are calculated:

a.   Q = 9; p = 8.5; TR = 76.5; TC = 36; profit = 40.5
b.   Market A:
        Q = 5 to 6; p = 9 to 10; TR = 50 to 54; TC = 20 to 24; profit = 30
    Market B:
        Q = 3 to 4; p = 7 to 8; TR = 24 to 28; TC = 12 to 16; profit = 12
        Combined profit = 42

If equations are used:

a.   Q = 9; p = 8.5; TR = 76.5; TC = 36; profit = 40.5
b.   Market A:
        Q = 5.5; p = 9.5; TR = 52.25; TC = 22; profit = 30.25
    Market B:
        Q = 3.5; p = 7.5; TR = 26.25; TC = 14; profit = 12.25
    Combined profit = 42.5

CHAPTER 13—CAPITAL BUDGETING

1.   The term "capital budgeting" refers to decisions

      a.   which are made in the short run.
      b.   which concern the spreading of expenditures over a period lasting less than one year.
*   c.   where expenditures and receipts for a particular undertaking will continue over a relatively long period of time.
      d.   where a receipt of cash will occur simultaneously with an outflow of cash.

2.   Capital budgeting projects include all of the following with the exception of

*   a.   the purchase of a six-month treasury bill.
      b.   the expansion of a plant.
      c.   the development of a new product.
      d.   the replacement of a piece of equipment.

3.   If $1,000 is placed in an account earning 8% annually, the balance at the end of seven years will be

      a. $1,080.
      b. $1,560.
      c. $2,000.
*   d. $1,714.

4.   The payback period for a project, requiring an initial outlay of $10,000 and producing ten uniform annual cash inflows of $1,500, is

      a.   six years.
*   b.   six years and eight months.
      c.   six years and six months.
      d.   seven years.

5.   The net present value of a project is calculated as follows:

      a.   the future value of all cash inflows minus the present value of all outflows.
      b.   the sum of all cash inflows minus the sum of all cash outflows.
*   c.   the present value of all cash inflows minus the present value of all cash outflows.
      d.   none of the above.

6.   The discount rate used to discount all the cash flows to the present is usually called

      a.   the cost of capital.
      b.   the internal rate of return.
      c.   the minimum required rate of return.
      d.   all of the above.
*   e.   a. and c. above.

7.   A proposed project should be accepted if the net present value is

*   a.   positive.
      b.   negative.
      c.   larger than the internal rate of return.
      d.   smaller than the internal rate of return.

8.   A project which requires an initial investment of $10,000 is expected to have annual cash flows of $2,800 each for the next five years. This project should be accepted if the cost of capital is

*   a.   12%.
      b.   13%.
      c.   14%.
      d   15%.

9.   A project which requires an initial investment of $10,000, is expected to have annual cash flows of $2,800 each for the next five years. This project should not be accepted if the cost of capital is

*   a.   13%.
      b.   12%.
      c.   11%.
      d.   10%.

10.   A project which requires an initial investment of $25,000, has the following for annual cash inflows:

Year	Cash Inflow
1	$5,000
2	8,000
3	12,000
4	8,000

      If the cost of capital is 12%, the present value of the cash inflows is

      a. $25,282, and the project can be accepted.
      b. $24,467, and the project can be accepted.
*   c. $24,467, and the project should be rejected.
      d. $25,282, and the project should be rejected.

11.   Other things being equal, the higher the cost of capital,

      a.   the higher the NPV of a project.
      b.   the higher the IRR of the project.
*   c.   the lower the NPV of the project.
      d.   the cost of capital has no effect on the NPV of the project.

12.   The internal rate of return of a project can be found

      a.   by discounting all cash flows at the cost of capital.
      b.   by averaging all cash inflows, and calculating the interest rate which will make them equal to the average investment.

*   c.   by calculating the interest rate which will equate the present value of all cash inflows to the present value of all cash outflows.
    d.   none of the above.

13.   A project with an initial investment of $30,000, and five equal annual cash inflows of $8,000, has an internal rate of return of

*   a.   10.4%.
    b.   10.0%.
    c.   11.2%.
    d.   11.5%.

14.   A project whose acceptance eliminates another project from consideration is called

    a.   independent.
*   b.   mutually exclusive.
    c.   replacement
    d.   complementary.

15.   The internal rate of return equals the cost of capital when

*   a.   NPV = 0
    b.   NPV > 0
    c.   NPV < 0
    d.   none of the above.

16.   When two mutually exclusive projects are considered, the NPV calculations and the IRR calculations may, under certain circumstances, give conflicting recommendations as to which project to accept. The reason for this result is that in the NPV calculation, cash inflows are assumed to be reinvested at the cost of capital, while in the IRR solution, reinvestment takes place at

    a.   the hurdle rate.
    b.   the accounting rate of return.
    c.   the prime rate.
*   d.   the project's internal rate of return.

17.   Writers of financial and economic literature generally recommend the use of NPV rather than IRR as the theoretically more correct technique because

    a.   the financial objective of the firm is the maximization of stockholder wealth, and the NPV measures the value of projects.
    b.   the IRR does not consider the size of the project.
    c.   the NPV reinvestment assumption is usually more realistic than the IRR assumption.
    d.   the dollar figure produced by NPV calculations is preferred to the percentage results of the IRR method by a majority of managers.
*   e.   a., b. and c. above.

18. When analyzing a capital budgeting project, the analyst must include in his calculation all of the following except:

    a. all revenues and costs in terms of cash flows.
    b. only those cash flows that will change if the proposal is accepted (i.e., incremental cash flows).
*   c. interest payments on debt financing connected with the project.
    d. any effect (impact) the acceptance of the project under consideration will have on other projects now in operation.

19. In considering a capital budgeting proposal, you estimate that cash sales during one of the years of the project will be $250, cash expenses (other than interest expense) will be $140, interest expense on the debt incurred $20, depreciation of the project's fixed assets $35, and the income tax rate 34%, how much will be the cash flow for that period?

Answer: $84.50
(250 - 140 - 35)*(.66) + 35 = 84.50

20. If, at the end of the project life, a piece of equipment having a book value of $3,000 is expected to bring $4,500 upon resale, and the income tax rate is 40%, how much will be the cash flow?

Answer: $3,900

21. If, at the end of the project life, a piece of equipment having a book value of $4,000 is expected to bring $3,000 upon resale, and the income tax rate is 40%, how much will be the cash flow?

Answer: $3,400

22. A piece of equipment was purchased for $20,000 and depreciated on a straight-line basis over 5 years to $0 book value at the end of five years. The company decides to sell this piece of equipment at the end of three years for $9,000. The income tax rate is 34%. The tax consequence of this transaction will be:

    a. a tax liability of $3,060.
    b. a tax refund of $340.
*   c. a tax liability of $340.
    d. a tax liability of $1,000.

23. A company purchased a machine for $100,000 four years ago. It was being depreciated on a straight-line basis over five years. The company decides to replace this machine today with a more productive machine which costs $125,000. The old machine can be sold today for $25,000. The income tax rate is 40%. The net initial investment in the new machine is

    a. $125,000.
    b. $100,000.
    c. $105,000.
*   d. $102,000.

24. An increase in net working capital required at the beginning of an expansion project must be considered to be

   a. a cash inflow.
   b. a reallocation of assets.
*   c. a cash outflow.
   d. none of the above.

25. If an expansion proposal is accepted, allowing an otherwise idle (and useless) machine with a market value and book value of $2,000 to be utilized, should it be recorded as a cash outflow, and if so, how much?

Answer: Yes, $2,000

26. A firm's most recent annual dividend was $2 per share; its shares sell for $40 in the stock market, and the company expects its dividend to grow at a constant rate of 5% in the foreseeable future. Using the dividend growth (Gordon) model, what would you estimate its equity cost of capital to be?

Answer: 10.25%
          (2)(1.05)/40 + .05

27. Usually, the cost of capital for newly issued stock is _____ the cost of retained earnings.

   a. lower than
*   b. higher than
   c. same as
   d. either higher or lower than

28. A stock whose rate of return fluctuates less than the rate of return of a market portfolio will have a beta which equals

   a. 1
*   b. less than 1.
   c. more than 1.
   d. either a. or c. above.

29. The equation for the required rate of return on an individual stock given by the Capital Asset Pricing Model is

   a. $k_j = R_f + \beta(R_f - k_m)$
   b. $k_j = R_f - \beta(k_m - R_f)$
*   c. $k_j = R_f + \beta(k_m - k_f)$
   d. $k_j = k_m + \beta(k_m - k_f)$

30. Company A has a beta of 1.3. The risk-free rate of interest is 6% and the rate of return on a market portfolio is 14%. Based on the Capital Asset Pricing Model, the required rate of return on Company A's stock should be

    a. 18.2%.
    b. 20%.
    c. 7.8%.
*   d. 16.4%.

31. A company's capital structure is made up of 40% debt and 60% common equity (both at market values). The interest rate on bonds similar to those issued by the company is 8%. The cost of equity is estimated to be 15%. The income tax rate is 40%. The company's weighted cost of capital is

    a. 11.5%.
    b. 12.2%.
*   c. 10.9%.
    d. 8.9%.

32. Capital rationing

    a. exists when a company sets an arbitrary limit on the amount of investment it is willing to undertake, so that not all projects with an NPV higher than the cost of capital will be accepted.
    b   generally does not permit a company to achieve maximum value.
    c. seems to occur quite frequently among corporations.
*   d. all of the above.

33. A company expects next year's free cash flow to be $800,000, and to grow at a rate of 7% in the foreseeable future. The company estimates its cost of capital to be 13%. The estimated value of this company is

*   a. $13,333,333.
    b. $6,153,846.
    c. $11,428,571.
    d. the data are insufficient to calculate an answer.

CHAPTER 14—RISK AND UNCERTAINTY

1. When future events cannot be assigned probabilities, we are talking about

     a. risk.
 *   b. uncertainty.
     c. a clouded future.
     d. financial risk.

2. Probabilities which can be obtained by repetition or are based on general mathematical principles are called

     a. statistical.
     b. empirical.
 *   c. a priori.
     d. subjective.

3. Probabilities which are based on past data or experience are called

     a. a priori.
     b. objective.
     c. uncertain.
 *   d. statistical.

4. In finance, risk is most commonly measured by

     a. the probability distribution.
 *   b. the standard deviation.
     c. the average deviation.
     d. the square root of the standard deviation.

5. When comparing two projects with different returns and different standard deviations, the risk measure which can be used is called the

     a. variance.
     b. certainty equivalent.
     c. coefficient of correlation.
 *   d. coefficient of variation.

6. One standard deviation above and below the expected value includes about

     a. 34% of the observations.
 *   b. 68% of the observations.
     c. 95% of the observations.
     d. 48% of the observations.

7. The risk adjusted discount rate

     a. is the sum of the risk-free rate and the risk premium.
     b. includes risk in the denominator of the present value calculation.

c.   includes risk in the numerator of the present value calculation.
d.   can be written as k = rf + RP.
*   e.   all except c. above.

8.   The use of the same cost of capital (risk adjusted discount rate) for all capital projects in a corporation

a.   is usually the correct procedure.
b.   is incorrect since different divisions of the corporation may be faced with different levels of risk.
c.   is incorrect since different capital projects, even in the same division, may be faced with different levels of risk.
*   d.   both b. and c.

9.   The XYZ Company has estimated expected cash flows for 1996 to be as follows:

Probability	Cash flow
.10	$120,000
.15	140,000
.50	150,000
.15	180,000
.10	210,000

Calculate

a.   expected value
b.   standard deviation
c.   coefficient of variation
d.   the probability that the cash flow will be less than $100,000.

Answers:

a. $156,000
b. $23,749
c.   0.152
d.   0.91% (z-statistic is 2.36)

10. You are given the following risky cash flows and certainty equivalent factors for a four-year project:

Period	Cash Flow	Certainty Equivalent Factor
1	$2,500	.95
2	3,000	.92
3	4,000	.88
4	3,000	.84

The initial investment for this project is $8,000, and the risk-free interest rate is 6%. Calculate the net present value of the project.

Answer: $1,648

11. If a risky cash flow of $10,000 is equivalent to a riskless cash flow of $9,300, the certainty equivalent factor is

*
    a. 0.93.
    b. 0.07.
    c. 1.07.
    d. 1.93.

12. If the risk adjusted discount rate method and the certainty equivalent methods are to give the same results, then the certainty equivalent factor (at) must equal (where rf is the risk-free interest rate, and k is the risk adjusted cost of capital)

    a. $(1 + r_f)^t$ times $(1 + k)^t$
    b. $(1 + k)^t$ divided by $(1 + r_f)^t$
*
    c. $(1 + r_f)^t$ divided by $(1 + k)^t$
    d. $(1 + k)^t$ minus $(1 + r_f)^t$

13. You are given risky cash flow data for a three-year project:

Year	Cash flow
1	$2,000
2	3,000
3	4,000

The initial cash outflow is $6,000; the risk-free interest rate is 6%, and the risk-adjusted discount rate is 10%.

Calculate the NPV by both the risk-adjusted discount rate method and the certainty equivalent method in such a way that the NPV will be the same using either method.-

Answer:

Year	Cash Flow	CE Factor*	Riskless Cash Flow	Riskless Cash Flow Discounted at 6%	Risky Cash Flow Discounted at 10%
1	2000	0.963636	1927	1818	1818
2	3000	0.928595	2786	2479	2479
3	4000	0.894828	3579	3005	3005
Total				7303	7303
Less initial investment				6000	6000
NPV				1303	1303

*CE factors:
1.06/1.1   = 0.963636
$1.06^2/1.1^2$ = 0.928595
$1.06^3/1.1^3$ = 0.894828

14.   Two projects have the following NPV's and standard deviations:

	Project A	*Project B*
NPV	200	200
Standard deviation	75	100

A person who selects project A over project B is

　　　a.   risk seeking.
　　　b.   risk indifferent.
*　　　c.   risk averse.
　　　d.   none of the above.

15.   Two projects have the following NPV's and standard deviations:

	Project A	*Project B*
NPV	200	300
Standard deviation	75	100

Which of the two projects is more risky?

Answer: Since the two projects have different NPV's and different standard deviations, relative risk can be measured by the coefficient of variation. Project A has a CV of .375, project B .333. Thus, the relative risk of project B is less.

16.   A source of business risk is

　　　a.   the firm's leverage.
　　　b.   general business conditions.
　　　c.   the firm finding an oil well on its property.
　　　d.   inflationary changes in costs.
*　　　e.   b. and d. above.

17.   The use of sensitivity analysis will generally result in

　　　a.   the calculation of a certainty equivalent NPV.
*　　　b.   the calculation of a best case, a base case and a worst case.
　　　c.   the calculation of the coefficient of variation.
　　　d.   the calculation of the probability of the maximum profit.

18.   Simulation analysis

*　　　a.   permits the calculation of expected value and standard deviation.
　　　b.   does not permit the calculation of expected value and standard deviation.
　　　c.   is too complex to ever be used in actual business situations.
　　　d.   does not consider probabilities.

19.   The expected value is

　　　a.   the total of all possible outcomes.
　　　b.   the arithmetic average of all possible outcomes.

*   c.   the average of all possible outcomes weighted by their respective probabilities.
      d.   the total of all possible outcomes divided by the number of different possible outcomes.

20.   A project has an expected NPV of $800, and a standard deviation of $300. It is almost certain that the actual NPV will turn out to be

      a.   no less that $-100.
      b.   no less than $200.
      c.   no more than $1,100.
      d.   no more than $1,700.
*   e.   both a. and d. above.

21.   A two-period project has the following probabilities and cash flows:

	Probability	Cash flow
Period 1:	.25	500
	.50	600
	.25	700
Period 2:	.30	300
	.50	500
	.20	700

The discount rate is 7%, and the initial investment is $1,000. How much is the expected NPV of this project?

Answer: $-20.

22.   An advantage of the decision tree is that

      a.   it eliminates the need for calculating the cost of capital.
      b.   it eliminates the need for calculating probabilities.
*   c.   it causes the analyst to consider important events that may occur in the course of the project, and decisions and actions that may have to be undertaken.
      d.   all of the above.

23.   A real option can present management with the opportunity to

      a.   vary output.
      b.   abandon a project.
      c.   postpone a project.
*   d.   all of the above.

24.   The use of real options in capital budgeting

*   a.   may raise the NPV of a capital project.
      b.   makes the analysis of the project considerably easier.
      c.   allows management to make decisions more quickly.
      d.   eliminates the need for calculating the project's risk adjusted discount rate.

CHAPTER 15—GOVERNMENT AND INDUSTRY

1. Which of the following is <u>not</u> considered a rationale for the intervention of government in the market process in the United States?

    a. the redistribution of income
    b. the reallocation of resources
*   c. the long run planning of scarce resources
    d. the short run stabilization of prices
    e. all of the above

2. Which of the following is the best example of a good or service that provides a benefit externality?

    a. the construction of a private road that allows vehicles if a toll is paid
*   b. a public library
    c. a bookstore that is open to everyone
    d. all of the above
    e. none of the above

3. Which of the following is <u>not</u> an example of a cost externality?

    a. the dumping of industrial waste into a lake
    b. unsightly billboards
    c. a neighbor that blasts his stereo system
*   d. the building of a new type of jet fighter bomber
    e. all of the above

4. The demand for products that provide benefit externalities is generally _____ the demand for products that do not.

    a. greater than
*   b. less than
    c. the same as
    d. greater or less (depending on the market) than

5. The supply for products that exhibit cost externalities is generally _____ the supply for products that do not.

*   a. greater than
    b. less than
    c. the same as
    d. greater or less (depending on the market) than

6. Which of the following is an example of a government action to internalize a cost externality?

*   a. a fine imposed on a company that pollutes a stream
    b. the closing of a public library
    c. a sales tax on jewelry
    d. the increase on bridge tolls

7.   When cost externalities exist, an optimal equilibrium can be attained if the government

     a.   restricts production.
     b.   levies a tax for the difference between private costs and social costs.
     c.   prohibits production.
     d.   all three above.
*   e.   both a. and b.

8.   The Coase theorem states that, in the presence of cost externalities, an optimal equilibrium can be attained

     a.   with government taxation.
     b.   by prohibiting production.
*   c.   by correctly defining property rights and through negotiation between the parties.
     d.   none of the above.

9.   Tying arrangements that lessen competition were made illegal by

     a.   the Sherman Anti-Trust Act.
*   b.   the Clayton Act.
     c.   the Celler-Kefauver Act.
     d.   the Robinson-Patman Act.

10. One school of anti-trust thought argues that, rather than ensuring efficiency, anti-trust laws are really aimed at

*   a.   protecting small independent firms against large corporations.
     b.   outlawing all monopolies whether they perform "bad acts" or not.
     c.   price differentiation due to differences in quality and cost.
     d.   restricting interlocking directorates.

11. Which of the following would <u>NOT</u> be considered a synergistic benefit from a merger?

     a.   an improvement in distribution systems
     b.   economies of scale in production
     c.   decreased cost of capital
*   d.   none of the above

12. A merger between two companies in unrelated fields of business

     a.   will always lead to economies of scale.
     b.   will generally increase the value of the unified firm compared to the value of the two companies before the merger because of the benefits of diversification.
*   c.   may not have any synergistic effects.
     d.   will necessarily lead to an increase in the market power of the merged company.